101 Crafts under $10

Easy-to-Make Ideas for Gifts and Home

101 Crafts under $10

Easy-to-Make Ideas for Gifts and Home

GUILDAMERICA
BOOKS®

FROM THE EDITORS AT BUTTERICK®

The Butterick® Publishing Company
161 Avenue of the Americas
New York, New York 10013

Editor: Trisha Malcolm

Book Editor: Julia Bernstein

Copy Editor: Annemarie McNamara

Managing Editors: Jean Guirguis, Stephanie Marracco

Designer: Chi Ling Moy

Illustrator: Elizabeth Berry

Contributing Editor: Colleen Mullaney Rotherham

Photography: Brian Kraus, Butterick Studios, NYC

Stylists: Christina Batch, Janet Rosell

Production Managers: Lillian Esposito, Winnie Hinish

President and CEO, Butterick® Company, Inc.: Jay H. Stein

Executive Vice President and Publisher, Butterick® Company, Inc.: Art Joinnides

Published by GuildAmerica Books™, an imprint and pending trademark of Doubleday Direct, Inc. licensed to BOOKSPAN.

1 3 5 7 9 10 8 6 4 2

Library of Congress Card Catalog Number: 99-052546

ISBN 1-57389-017-0 (hardcover)

contents

Photo: VNU/Dennis Brandsma

ten dollars does not seem like a large amount of money to spend making a truly original accessory or gift item. Even better, when you look through your craft supplies, and then consider all of the plain and unadorned items lying around your home, you may not need to spend even a penny! This book will show you how to easily and affordably transform uninspired objects and throwaways into one-of-a-kind creations.

There were a few assumptions made when determining the cost for the projects in this book. First of all, instead of purchasing items brand-new, we found used items around the home to renew. If you do not happen to have a frame, lamp or pillow in need of a facelift, scout flea markets, garage sales and second-hand stores for inexpensive items to update. The prices assigned are also based on the belief that you already have most of the tools shown in our craft tool kit. While having to purchase these would significantly increase the price of your project, the investment will more than pay for itself over time. Sometimes, it would cost more than ten dollars to buy all of the supplies for a project, even though less than ten dollars worth of materials were used. In these cases, we suggest using leftovers, such as fabric scraps. In addition, prices given refer to making a single item unless otherwise stated. If you choose to make multiple items, such as cards and gift bags, the price will increase accordingly.

All of the frames used were recycled. To prepare old frames for decorating, gently sand the surfaces and wipe them clean. With paint, fabric or découpage, old surfaces can look new again. Candles are a great way to create a tranquil mood both in and outdoors. Instead of buying new candles, dress up plain candles you have around the home. With a little paint or by applying found objects, you can create a stunning decorative accent. Pillows are also great for giving a room a new outlook. There's no need to purchase a pillow form—simply stuff an old throw pillow into a fresh cover. You can use fabric remnants from home decorating projects, or try recycling old denims or scraps of felt.

In addition to choosing a project according to your likes and needs, you should also consider what materials you have on hand. Old table linens can be salvaged and made into pillows and place mats, while a torn quilt can be rescued and made into charming country-style pot holders. Even items you normally throw away, like cardboard rolls from paper towels, shoeboxes, oatmeal containers and pretzel tins, can be cleverly transformed into attractive and fun items for you and your family to enjoy. Often, the materials used for a project can be substituted with comparable items. For example, instead of washers, you can stitch buttons on a pillow cover; instead of making a mosaic frame from tiles, use shells or pebbles you've gathered outdoors.

So, think twice before you toss it out! With a little creativity, you can give throwaways and flea market finds a new lease on life.

frames & photos

handcrafted frames are as delightful and decorative as the items displayed inside. Adapt frames according to your likes and the needs of the artwork exhibited.

weathered hardware frame

Fashion a frame from everyday materials found in the workroom. Rows of nails and upholstery tacks combine with a crackled surface to give this frame a rustic look.

materials

- flat-faced wooden picture frame
- upholstery tacks
- ½"/1.3cm nails
- acrylic paint: dark brown & rust
- acrylic crackle medium
- matte acrylic varnish
- wash paintbrush
- hammer

Note: Allow each coat of paint/medium to dry thoroughly before applying next. The quantity of tacks/nails will vary according to size of frame.

1. Paint frame with rust-colored paint. Follow manufacturer's guidelines to apply crackle medium, then dark brown paint. Finish with coat of acrylic varnish.

2. Hammer same number of upholstery tacks to each frame corner on diagonal. Hammer nails to border and inside edge of frame, approximately ¼"/6mm apart.

$ 1-5

cluster-frame album cover

Keep special memories in an album with its own multi-frame cover. Choose photos that will let you know at a glance the occasion commemorated inside.

materials

- photo album
- sheet of medium-weight decorative paper at least 1"/2.5cm larger all around than album cover (front and back)
- sheet of lightweight paper in contrasting color (colored stationery works well)
- specialty scissors with contoured edges
- découpage medium & spongebrush
- ⅛"/3mm rope trim & white craft glue
- black and white copies of photos (reduce 4" x 6"/10cm x 15cm photos 50% or 65%)

1. Lay photo album out flat with cover side facing up. Follow manufacturer's guidelines to apply découpage medium to one side of medium-weight paper. Center paper over album and smooth in place, wrapping edges around to inside. When paper is almost dry, gently close album cover.

2. Use black and white copies as is or trim into squares, rounds or ovals. Using specialty scissors, cut a piece of lightweight paper ⅛"/3mm larger all around than each photo.

3. Arrange colored papers on cover. Apply medium to one side of paper and smooth in place. Center photos over colored papers. Apply medium to wrong side and smooth in place. Repeat this process for spine and back cover. When dry, apply coat of medium over entire album.

4. Glue rope trim around edges of album.

$$ 6-10

An elaborate frame isn't best suited to everything you'd like to display. Two simple hinged wooden frames show off photos without a lot of frills or fuss.

materials

- 2 identical flat-faced frames
- 8 hinges (size will depend on size of frames)
- acrylic paint: dark brown & rust
- acrylic crackle medium
- matte acrylic varnish
- wash paintbrush
- screwdriver

Note: Allow each coat of paint/medium to dry thoroughly before applying next.

1. Paint frames dark brown and let dry. Follow manufacturer's guidelines to apply crackle medium, then rust-colored paint. Finish with coat of acrylic varnish.

2. Attach a hinge to outer corners of each frame, then join frames together with four hinges at center.

$ 1-5

embellished frames

Display favorite snapshots in whimsical frames decorated with craft foam scenery and marvelous miniature objects.

materials

- 3½" x 5"/9cm x 12.5cm flat-faced wooden picture frame
- sheets of fun foam: green, blue & white
- acrylic paint: silver, black & white
- paintbrushes: round & spotter
- white craft glue
- for fishing frame: 2 miniature fish: 2 wood skewers; cotton cord; paper clips & candle cup; for garden frame: silk leaves; mini clay pots; paper flowers & miniature bridge
- scissors

Note: Miniatures can be purchased at craft, hobby, doll and baking supply stores.

1. To make fishing frame, paint frame in desired background color and let dry. Cut water, grass and clouds from fun foam and glue in place. Paint candle cup silver and let dry.

2. Arrange miniatures on frame, extending over inside and outside edges. Make fishing poles from skewers and cord, with pieces of paper clip for hook. Use candle cup for bucket with pieces of paper clip for handle. Glue pieces in place.

3. Paint details such as birds in sky and bubbles in water with spotter. Follow the same method to make garden frame.

$$ 6-10

Multi-looped patterned ribbon bows add charm to wallpaper-covered frames. If desired, a more elaborate bow can be sculpted using wire-edged ribbon.

materials

- picture frame
- wallpaper
- découpage medium & spongebrush
- 1½yds/1.40m ribbon
- all-purpose glue gun & glue sticks
- scissors

1. Cut a piece of wallpaper 2"/5cm larger all around than frame. Follow product guidelines to apply découpage medium to wallpaper. Center paper over frame and smooth in place, wrapping outside edges around to back. Cut diagonally from center of frame opening to inside corners. Wrap inside edges of paper around to back of frame and trim excess. Seal paper with two or three coats medium. Let each coat dry before applying next.

2. Cut two lengths of ribbon, one 3"/7.5cm shorter than the other. Form each length into loop and glue ends together. Cut short length of ribbon. With smaller loop centered over larger one, tie loops together in center to make bow. Glue bow to top center of frame. Cut remaining length of ribbon in two equal pieces. Glue each piece to either side of bow, slipping ends under bottom loop. Fold ribbons around corners and sides of frame, gluing folds as you go. Trim ends.

$ 1-5

baby keepsake box

Safely store your dear one's cherishables in a box lovingly adorned with decorative papers and topped with a framed photo.

materials

- cardboard shoebox
- assorted wrapping papers
- découpage medium & spongebrush
- 3½" x 5"/9cm x 12.5cm wooden picture frame
- acrylic paint & round paintbrush
- pinking shears or specialty scissors with contoured edges
- 2yds/1.85m ½"/1.3cm-wide ribbon
- all-purpose glue gun & glue sticks or white craft glue

1. Follow manufacturer's guidelines to apply découpage medium to shoebox, covering outside of box and lid. Cover box and lid with paper.

2. Cut out patches and/or motifs from papers with specialty scissors and découpage onto background. Pieces can be layered or overlapped, as desired. Allow box and lid to dry.

3. Paint picture frame with two coats paint in coordinating color.

4. Wrap length of ribbon around sides of box lid and glue in place. Tie remaining ribbon into bow. Glue bow to one corner of frame, then glue ribbon tails trailing along borders.

5. Place picture in frame. Glue frame to top of box.

 free

Plant a cheery flower garden blooming with all of your friends' faces. Set the flower frames in a pot painted with matching motifs.

materials

- approx. 3"/7.5cm-diameter clay pot with tray
- acrylic paint: yellow, brown & green
- floral stems (as many as desired)
- Spanish moss
- 1yd/.95m gold cord
- paper glue, all-purpose glue gun & glue sticks
- Styrofoam (to fit inside pot)
- photographs & lightweight cardboard
- round paintbrush, clean new pencil eraser & toothpick

1. Paint cardboard brown. Cut 1¾"/4.5cm circles from cardboard. If photographs are the right size, use them as is. If not, make color copies to size. Cut out faces from background and center on cardboard circles. Use paper glue to glue in place. Glue gold cord around each photo circle, then glue circles on flower centers.

2. Dip eraser in brown paint and stamp flower centers around border of pot, leaving space in between for petals. Let dry. Clean eraser, then stamp yellow petals around centers. With toothpick, drag paint out to edges to create petal shapes. Paint green leaves with brush. Let dry.

3. Glue gold cord around edge of tray and bottom of painted border on pot.

4. Glue pot to center of tray. Glue Styrofoam inside pot. Trim stems and insert in foam. Glue moss over foam.

$ 1-5

cracked china frame

Salvage chipped and cracked china pieces by using them to resurface plain frames. Scour yard sales and flea markets for old dishes to shatter and use for decoration.

materials

- flat-faced picture frame with approx. 1½"/3.8cm-wide border
- ceramic plates
- ceramic tile mastic & premixed tile grout
- craft stick, sponge & tack cloth
- hammer, plastic bag, towel & safety glasses

1. Place plate in plastic bag, then wrap towel around bag. Wearing safety glasses, crack plates with hammer. Remove towel to check if plates are in small enough pieces. Repeat process as above until pieces are broken into sizes that fit within width of frame border.

2. Carefully remove pieces from bag and lay them out on a flat surface. Begin laying pieces on frame without adhering. Leave approximately ⅛"/3mm between pieces. If width (depth) of border is wide enough, place ceramic pieces around width as well.

3. With stick, apply generous coating of tile mastic to wrong side of ceramic pieces. Set in place and allow to dry completely.

4. Follow manufacturer's guidelines to apply tile grout. Polish completed frame with soft cloth.

$ 1-5

accordion frame

Picture mats come in a variety of sizes with different shaped openings. Join three mats together and decorate with fabric and trim to make an attractive fold-out frame.

materials
- three 5" x 7"/12.5cm x 18cm picture mats
- cardboard (if not included with mat)
- 3⅓yds/3.1m braided trim
- 1⅓yds/1.3m string of pearls
- ½yd/.5m ⅜"/1cm-wide satin ribbon
- 3 ribbon roses
- white craft glue
- white cloth or adhesive tape, ¾"/2cm wide
- scissors

1. If not included, cut a piece of cardboard the same size as each mat. Glue cardboard to mats along three outside edges, leaving top open to slip photos through. Let glue dry. Lay mats side by side on a flat surface, leaving about ¹⁄₁₆"/1.5mm between mats. Lay strips of tape centered over spaces between mats on both front and back sides. (This will allow mats to be gently folded.)
2. Glue trim around openings in mats and around outside edges of mats, covering tape. Glue pearls around trim at openings.
3. Cut ribbon into three equal pieces. Tie ribbon pieces into small bows. Glue bows at top center of openings. Glue ribbon rose at center of each bow.
$$ 6-10

shadow box displays

Heirlooms and other articles long stored in bureau drawers can be framed and hung for unique wall accents.

materials

Note: Materials for this project will depend on size of frame selected. We suggest using a frame no smaller than 8" x 10"/20.5cm x 25.5cm. Frame used for project shown is 11" x 14"/28cm x 35.5cm.

- wood picture frame
- ¼"/6mm plywood (bottom of box)
- 1 x 3 pine (sides of box)
- wood glue
- white craft glue
- silicone glue

- 2 metal hinges & 1 metal hook and eye
- sandpaper
- cardboard
- quilt batting
- fabric
- white acrylic primer
- 2 colors of acrylic paint
- crackle medium
- wash paintbrush
- acrylic varnish
- handsaw

1. Measure length and width of picture frame at outside edges. Cut plywood to this size for bottom of box. Cut pine into four lengths equal to edges of frame (2 pieces cut to length of frame and 2 pieces cut to width of frame less the width of length strips). **Note**: Many lumberyards will gladly cut plywood and pine to size for a small fee.

2. Glue strips to plywood with wood glue and allow glue to dry. Sand "box" and frame to prepare for painting (remove easel backing and glass from frame). Apply acrylic primer to both pieces and let dry. Apply one color of acrylic paint (this is the color that will show through cracks after medium dries). Follow manufacturer's guidelines to apply crackle medium. Apply second color of paint as directed.

When paint is dry, apply acrylic varnish to seal and protect box.

3. To line box, cut pieces of cardboard ⅜"/1cm smaller all around than each side and back of box. Glue a piece of batting to each piece of cardboard. Cut a piece of fabric ½"/1.3cm larger all around than each piece of cardboard. Center fabric over cardboard and wrap fabric around to back side, gluing in place. Glue back piece in first, then sides.

4. Use silicone glue to glue glass to frame (easel and backing can be discarded or saved for another project). Join frame, which is the door to your box, to box with hinges on one side. Attach metal hook and eye to other side to hold box closed.

$$ 6-10

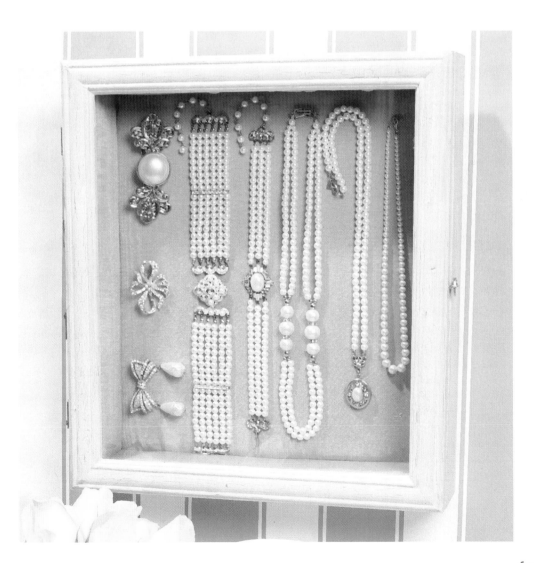

mosaic tile frame

Small, glazed tiles give this clay-based frame a unique appearance. Place matching tiles in neat rows or mix and match colored tiles for a lively look.

materials

- flat-faced wooden picture frame
- small, square glazed tiles
- off-white air-dry clay
- contact cement
- tack cloth

Note: Use broken tiles purchased from tile store or leftovers from home improvement project. Follow the same simple method to decorate frames with seashells and pebbles.

1. Remove backing and glass from frame. Press ⅜"/1cm-thick layer of clay on front and edges of frame.

2. Coat backs of tiles with contact cement. Press tiles into clay to cover frame, leaving ⅛"/3mm spaces between pieces.

3. Use cloth to polish surface of tiles. Air-dry to set clay.

 $$ 6-10

metallic frame

Give objects a glittering finish in a sparkling metallic frame. This painted-silver frame is grand enough to display precious heirlooms and vintage photos.

materials

- wooden picture frame (single frame or multiple-hinged frames)
- acrylic paint: metallic silver & black
- round paintbrush
- fine sandpaper
- tack cloth

1. Sand frame to prepare to receive paint. Wipe off dust with cloth.

2. Base-coat frame black and let dry.

3. Paint frame with two coats metallic silver paint, letting paint dry between coats. After paint has dried, lightly rub all over frame with fine sandpaper to expose some of the base color.

$ 1-5

creative candles

everyone loves the tranquil ambiance created by flickering candlelight. Decorating candles is quick and easy, yet the results are always impressive. Custom-design candles to fill your home with warmth and beauty.

Nothing enhances votive candles more beautifully than natural materials gathered outdoors. Spice up your décor with a cinnamon stick-covered candle tied with a raffia bow.

materials

- 3 votive candles
- tree bark
- all-purpose glue gun & glue sticks

1. Glue all three candles together.
2. Break tree bark into small pieces and glue around base of candles, slightly overlapping pieces. Glue second layer of slightly smaller bark pieces over first, overlapping edges.

$ free

materials

- approx. 2"/5cm diam., 3½"/9cm tall candle
- cinnamon sticks
- natural raffia
- all-purpose glue gun & glue sticks
- scissors

1. Glue cinnamon sticks in tight row around candle. Height of sticks can be varied by carefully trimming with scissors.
2. Twist several strands of raffia together and tie around candle with bow on front.

$ 1-5

beaded wire candle ring

Thread silver beads on coiled wire to make a sparkling collar for a pillar. Set the candle in a gilded holder for an elegant effect.

materials

- candle
- 14 gauge colored copper wire
- beads (holes must be large enough to be threaded onto wire)
- white craft glue
- wire cutter & needle-nose pliers
- broomstick
- tape measure

1. This candle decoration can be made for any size candle. To determine length of wire needed, measure circumference of candle and multiply by five. (For example, our candle has a 12"/30.5cm circumference, multiplied by five equals 5'/152.5cm.)

2. Wrap entire length of wire firmly around broomstick, then remove.

3. Thread beads onto wire, approximately 1½"/3.8cm apart. Use small drop of glue to keep beads from shifting on wire.

4. Use needle-nose pliers to make two small loops from scraps of wire. Bring ends of coiled wire together to form ring. Slip ends of coiled wire through loops to hold ring together.

$ 1-5

flower blossom candles

Candles in all sizes come alive stenciled with pretty pink flowers. Choose flat surface candles to make painting easier.

materials
- candles
- acrylic paint: fuschia, medium green, dark green & yellow
- candle painting medium
- small pieces of sponge
- tracing paper & pencil
- acetate & craft knife
- paintbrushes: liner & angular shader
- toothpick
- fine point permanent marker

1. To make "stencils," trace flower and leaf pattern onto tracing paper. Cut two 2½"/6.5cm squares of acetate, one for flower pattern and one for leaf. Place acetate over tracing paper pattern and trace outlines with marker. Use craft knife to cut out stencils.

2. Mix acrylic paints with candle painting medium following instructions on package. Hold stencil on surface of candle. Moisten sponge and wring dry. Dab sponge in paint and apply paint through stencil openings, using pink for flowers and two shades of green for leaves. Leaves and flowers can be used separately or clustered, as desired. Let dry. Dip tip of toothpick in yellow paint and dot center of flowers. Use liner brush to paint leaf stems and veins. Paint small leaves freehand with angular shader brush.

 6-10

flower

leaf

corded candlesticks

Ordinary cord adds unique beauty and texture coiled around a simple pair of candlesticks.

materials

- smooth-surface candlesticks
- non-stretch cord or string
- old, stiff paintbrush
- tacky white glue
- scissors

1. Starting at bottom, use brush to apply glue in 1"/2.5cm sections. Cut end of cord at angle. Press end on bottom side of base. Begin wrapping cord around base, concealing end with first row. Hold cord in place until glue begins to set, 10 to 20 seconds.

2. Continue in same manner, applying sections of glue and wrapping cord until entire candlestick is covered. Press each row snug against the next and make sure there are no gaps. Trim end at angle and tuck beneath previous row.

$ 1-5

blooming beeswax candle

Molded beeswax and a sky blue pillar come together to make a pretty flowering candle that would lighten up any room of the house.

materials

- pillar, approx. 3"/7.5cm diameter, 9"/23cm tall
- 12" x 8"/30.5cm x 20.5cm sheets of beeswax: yellow & light blue
- craft knife & ruler
- white craft glue

Note: Keep candle and beeswax at room temperature. Beeswax will crack if it is too cold. Hands should be clean, dry and warm for best results.

1. Cut beeswax into 8" x ¼"/20.5cm x 6mm strips. Roll beeswax into circles. For each daisy, you will need one light blue circle and five yellow circles. Polka dots are blue circles. Gently press circles together to form flowers.

2. Apply a thin layer of glue to back of each flower and polka dot and press against candle. Hold in place until glue sets. Continue gluing on flowers and dots until entire candle is covered in a pleasing and balanced pattern.

$$ 6-10

holly berry candle

Spread holiday warmth and cheer by decorating a red pillar with golden leaves and berries.

materials
- approx. 3"/7.5cm-diameter, 9"/23cm-tall candle
- pine spray
- artificial (silk) holly & other winter greenery
- gold spray paint & newspaper
- all-purpose glue gun & glue sticks

Note: Carefully follow manufacturer's guidelines when working with spray paint.

1. Spread leaves and pine on newspaper and spray paint. Allow time to dry, turn over, and paint other side.

2. Glue larger, then smaller leaves around base of candle, standing vertically and slightly overlapping edges. Glue pine around bottom edge of candle. Glue berries over pine.

 free

ribboned candle garden

Make a lovely candle garden to brighten your home! Wrap white pillars with satin ribbons, decorate with stamped wax, then group on a tray or serving table.

materials

- white pillars in assorted sizes
- sealing wax in desired colors
- wax stamp or found objects, such as a buttons or dice
- satin ribbons in assorted colors and widths
- white craft glue
- scissors

1. Wrap ribbon casually around candle as many times as desired, leaving long trailing ends. Overlap ends diagonally and secure in place with glue.

2. Heat sealing wax by turning it over lit candle. Drip sufficient amount of melted wax over joint where ribbon ends overlap. Working quickly, press stamp or object firmly down in melted wax. Hold stamp in place until wax hardens, then remove to reveal impression. Trim ribbon ends as desired.

Note: Be careful not to let candles burn within one inch of the ribbon.

$$ 6-10

monogrammed candle cups

Personalize a collection of frosted candle cups with paint and purchased stencils. Initial cups for each family member or have them spell out a special greeting.

materials
- frosted drinking glasses
- white tealights
- gold glass paint
- alphabet stencil (flexible enough to fit snugly around curved glass)
- tape
- stencil brush
- paper towels

1. Position letter stencil on center side of glass and tape in place.

2. Dip brush in paint and dab on paper towel to remove excess. Apply paint through stencil opening. Use light touch to glide paint on smooth surface; let dry.

3. Remove stencil and wipe thoroughly clean. Position second initial next to first, making sure top and bottom edges are even; tape in place. Stencil letter in same manner as first, letting paint dry before removing stencil. Place tealight in glass.

$$ 6-10

shiny candle pots

Miniature clay pots sponged silver and gold combine with gold beads and long elegant tapers to create a stunning duo.

materials
- two 1½"/3.8cm clay pots with trays
- acrylic paint: silver, gold & color to match tapers
- round paintbrush
- small piece of sponge
- small gold beads
- Spanish moss
- all-purpose glue gun & glue sticks
- 2 tapers

1. Paint pot and tray with silver paint; let dry. Lightly sponge on paint color to match tapers. Let dry, then sponge with gold paint.

2. Glue pot to tray, then glue small gold beads around rim of pot.

3. Glue candle to bottom of pot and surround with Spanish moss.

$$ 6-10

seashell candle stands

A candle stand of glistening shells set on a wooden base is an ideal way to add natural beauty and warmth to a summer home or outdoor gathering.

Photo: VNU/Luuk Geertsen

materials

- wooden block approx. 3"/7.5cm-square
- assorted shells, unbroken
- candle
- all-purpose glue gun & glue sticks
- small sharp knife & tack cloth

1. Scrape away barnacles and other build-up from shells with knife. Rub off surface sand and dirt with damp cloth. If desired, whiten discolored shells by soaking in solution of one part chlorine bleach to four parts water. Dry wet shells thoroughly.

2. If wood block does not have circular recess, draw circle in center top of block. Glue ring of shells to wood base, following outline of circle. Glue second ring of shells on top of first. Vary placement and position of shells for interest. Hold each shell in place and wait for glue to set before moving on to next. Place candle in center of ring.

$ free

carved ivy candle

Transform a plain candle into a work of art by sponging on layers of green paint and carving a winding ivy pattern.

materials

- ivory candle
- acrylic paint: light, medium & dark green
- candle painting medium
- small piece of sponge
- linoleum cutting tool
- stylus
- tracing paper & pencil

1. Trace vine pattern on tracing paper. Pattern can be enlarged or reduced on a copy machine, depending on size of candle, or vine lengths can be connected to decorate larger candle. Lay pattern on candle and use stylus to "emboss" pattern on surface of candle.

2. Mix acrylic paints with candle painting medium, following instructions on package. Wet sponge and wring dry. Sponge medium shade of green paint on surface of candle. Let dry, then apply lighter shade of green. Sponge on darkest shade of green once lighter shade has dried. The surface of the candle should have a variegated appearance. Allow to dry thoroughly before carving.

3. Use linoleum cutters to carefully carve stems and leaves following "embossed" pattern. Cut through outer painted layer just deep enough to expose ivory candle.

$$ 6-10

paper is a wonderfully versatile medium for all sorts of craft projects. In no time at all, you can make impressive objects to beautify your home and original and personal gifts for friends and family.

Transform everyday stationery into something truly special! Enliven the borders of plain sheets of paper with delicate pressed flowers in a spectrum of garden colors.

materials

- pressed flowers & leaves
- 8½" x 11"/21.8cm x 28cm sheets of stationery or pieces of decorative paper cut to size*
- découpage medium
- paintbrush & fine-tipped marker
- tweezers & cotton swab

* for decorative paper use: straight ruler, pencil, specialty scissors with contour edges or rotary cutter

Note: Dry flowers with purchased flower-press or hand-press flowers between sheets of absorbent paper weighted with heavy books.

1. If using decorative paper, use ruler and pencil to mark dimensions on wrong side. Use a rotary cutter or specialty scissors to cut out sheet. Edges can be straight, shaped or combination of both.

2. Arrange dried flowers and leaves on paper. With tweezers or your fingers, carefully lift flowers and leaves one at a time and use cotton swab to lightly apply tiny dabs of découpage medium on back. Gently press flower/leaf in place and smooth with swab. Continue in same manner gluing flowers and leaves to paper until composition is complete. To finish, apply a thin coat of découpage medium over flowers. If desired, add stems and vines with marker.

$ 1-5

fruity mosaic tray

Turn a plain serving tray into a mosaic masterpiece. Simply tear and piece paper shapes together to form a kaleidoscope of brightly colored fruits.

materials

- found serving tray
- spray paint in dark color
- découpage medium
- paintbrushes: liner & sponge
- assorted sheets of colored stationery: yellow, orange, chartreuse, green, violet, red, burgundy & black
- graphite paper & pencil
- scissors

1. Enlarge pattern on photocopier to fit tray. Use graphite paper to transfer shapes to sheets of paper, referring to illustration for colors.

2. Carefully tear shapes from papers. If desired, dampen liner brush with small amount of water and lightly paint over lines before tearing.

3. Spraypaint tray in background color of choice. Follow paint manufacturer's guidelines for safe usage. Let dry thoroughly.

4. Using spongebrush, follow manufacturer's guidelines to apply découpage medium to papers. Position each piece of paper on tray and smooth in place before moving on to next. Allow first layer of mosaic pieces to dry before applying next layer. Apply two to three topcoats of découpage medium after all mosaic pieces are in place.

$ 1-5

materials

- heavyweight decorative paper
- tracing paper, graphite paper & pencil
- white craft glue
- scoring tool (the tip of a small crochet hook works well) or stylus
- scissors
- ribbon

1. Enlarge pattern to size on photocopier. Envelope can be made small or large as desired to fit lightweight gift items such as jewelry, scarves or ties.

2. Trace pattern onto tracing paper, then use graphite paper to transfer pattern to wrong side of decorative paper.

3. Cut out pattern along outside edges. Score, then gently fold all pattern lines.

4. Fold envelope on straight lines. Apply glue to right side of narrow strip on top. Fold strip down, bring envelope around, and glue in place. Allow glue to dry completely, then fold in oval ends. Tie package with ribbon bow.

$ 1-5

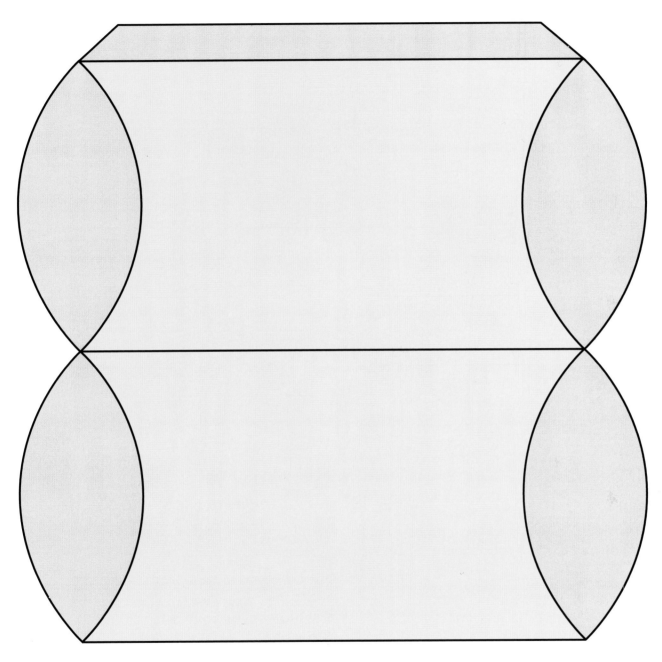

enlarge 118%

fancy jewelry boxes

Recycle old greeting cards to make one-of-
a-kind gift boxes. Though inexpensive to
make, these lovely containers give gifts an
elegant finale.

materials

- greeting cards
- tracing paper, graphite paper & pencil
- white craft glue
- scoring tool (the tip of a small crochet hook
  works well) or stylus
- straightedge scissors & specialty scissors
  with contour edges

1. Enlarge pattern to size on photocopier.
Size of box cannot exceed size of greeting
card being used. Top of box will be front of
card; bottom will be back of card.

2. Trace pattern onto tracing paper, then
use graphite paper to transfer patterns to
wrong side of greeting card front and back
as indicated (wrong side is side that will
be folded in to form box).

3. Cut out patterns along outside edges.
This can be done with straight or contour-
edged scissors. Score all solid lines. Follow
dotted lines to cut out triangular shapes
with scissors. Gently fold lines.

4. Fold pieces in to form box top and bottom with triangular flap folded to the
inside. Apply glue to hold corners in place.
Slip top over bottom.

$ free

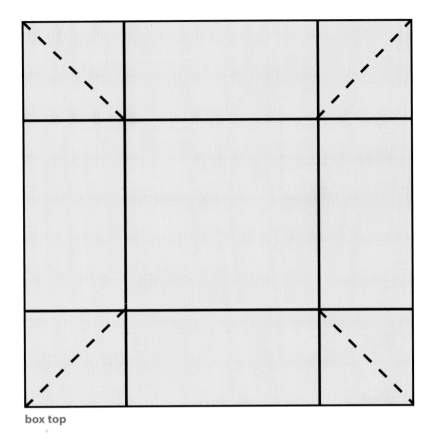

box top

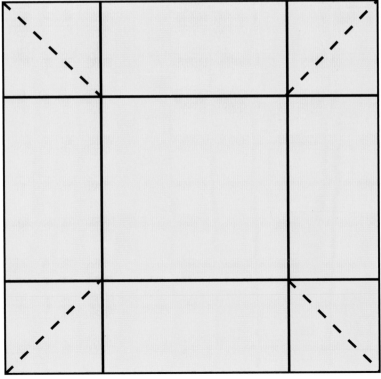

box bottom

pretty paper portfolio

Keep stationery neatly organized in a handsome portfolio. Made from sheets of decorative paper, this holder is attractive enough to display on a desktop or table.

materials

- 1 sheet of medium-weight decorative paper, 15" x 23"/38cm x 58.5cm
- 1 sheet of heavyweight decorative paper, 20" x 20"/51cm x 51cm
- paper glue & white craft glue
- 6 wood buttons
- jute twine
- ruler & pencil
- scissors or craft knife

1. Cut one 14" x 21"/35.5cm x 53.5cm and one 13" x 1½"/33cm x 3.8cm piece of paper from medium-weight sheet. Cut two 9½" x 13"/24.3cm x 33cm and two 9½" x 6½"/24.3cm x 16.3cm pieces of paper from heavyweight sheet.

2. On wrong side (or either side if both sides are identical), draw pencil line ½"/1.3cm all around on 14" x 21"/35.5cm x 53.5cm sheet of paper for portfolio cover.

3. Place one 9½" x 6½"/24.3cm x 16.3cm piece of paper on top of one 9½" x 13"/24.3cm x 33cm piece of paper, right sides up and matching bottom edges, for portfolio pocket. Do same with other two pieces of paper for second pocket.

4. Line one set of pocket papers along left side of pencil line on large sheet of paper. Fold left edge of cover paper in along pencil line and glue in place on pocket papers. Do same on right side with other set of pocket papers. Next, fold top and bottom edges of cover paper in along pencil line and glue in place, mitering corners.

5. Glue 1½" x 13"/3.8cm x 33cm strip of medium-weight paper centered over inside edges of pocket. Fold holder in half so that pockets are on inside.

6. Thread a 12"/30.5cm length of twine in each of two buttons. Glue buttons to center side front and back of holder. Use twine to tie holder closed. Embellish front of holder with remaining buttons and twine, as shown in illustration.

$$ 6-10

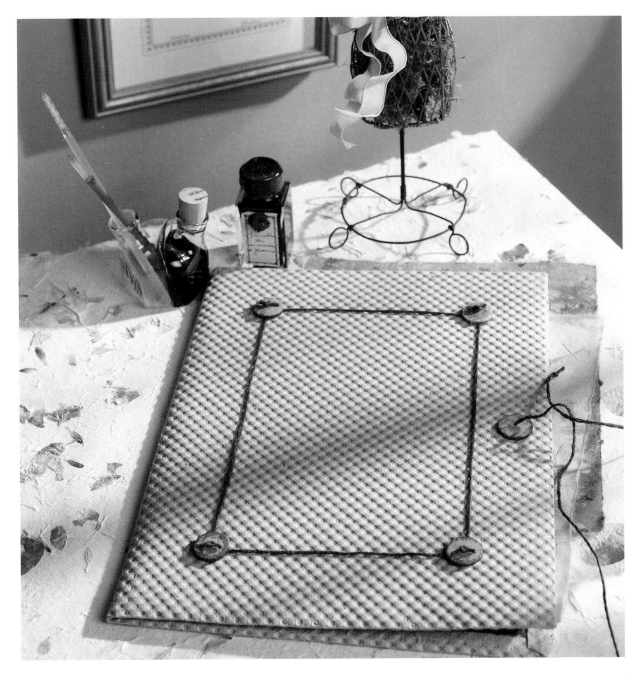

embossed envelopes

Heartfelt messages are made even more meaningful when delivered in an elegant handmade embossed envelope.

materials

- envelopes with large flaps
- small pieces of craft foam
- white craft glue
- tracing paper, graphite paper, pencil & masking tape
- scissors
- wood craft stick or burnisher
- water & paintbrush

1. Trace pattern onto tracing paper. Place pattern over foam with graphite paper in between and outline all shapes. Cut out all shapes, as indicated on template (see opposite page).

2. Cut out 4"/10cm square piece of foam. Glue shapes onto foam square to make embossing "plate."

3. On right side (outside) of envelope flap, use paintbrush to moisten area to be embossed. Place "plate" with right side against moist area and tape in place.

4. Turn flap to wrong side and with craft stick or burnisher, begin gently rubbing over plate. (You can use your fingers to feel the recessed areas of the plate.) Continue rubbing over plate until all recessed areas are sharp and clear. Run burnisher or craft stick along edge of frame on plate to create border.

5. Remove plate and allow paper to dry.

$ 1-5

cut out beige areas

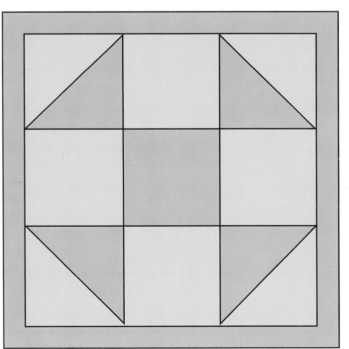

handmade gift bags

Don't settle for bland, store-bought bags!
Custom-design your own gift-bags to
delight and surprise all of your friends.

- 8½" x 11"/21.8cm x 28cm sheet of medium-weight paper
- paper glue
- 12"/30.5cm-long piece of ⅛"/3mm-wide ribbon
- rubber stamp & ink pad
- tracing paper, pencil, ruler & graphite paper
- scissors or craft knife
- large needle

1. Enlarge pattern to size on photocopier. Trace bag pattern onto tracing paper. Place tracing over medium-weight paper with graphite paper in between. Transfer pattern to paper, then cut out along outside edges using scissors or craft knife.

2. Fold top down along fold line and glue in place. (All fold lines will be on the inside of the bag.)

3. Stamp pattern on outside of bag. Pattern can be random or planned.

4. Fold all vertical lines towards inside of bag. Fold bottom up along horizontal line. Form bag by overlapping wide panel over narrow one and gluing in place. Fold ends in, then sides, and glue in place.

5. Cut piece of ribbon in half. Pierce two pairs of holes at top of bag with large needle. Thread ends of ribbon through holes from outside to inside of bag and knot ends to make handles.

$ 1-5

enlarge pattern 140%

top

fold lines

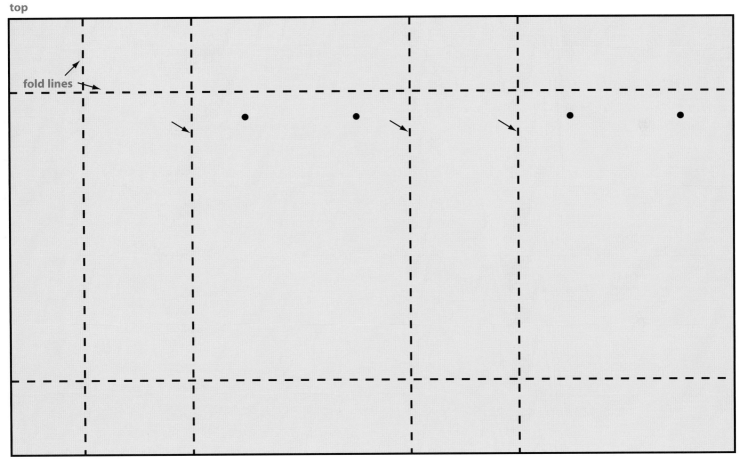

bottom

fantasy feline boxes

There's no need for useful objects to be dull. With a little paint and paper, a stack of round papier mâché boxes becomes a practical and fun kitty-cat storage solution.

materials

- three oval papier mâché boxes, approx. 3½", 4½", 5½"/9cm, 11.5cm, 14cm
- 4" x 6"/10cm x 15cm piece of heavy paper or lightweight cardboard
- acrylic paints: light grey, dark grey, white, pink, light green & black
- paintbrushes: liner, round & stencil
- two ½"/1.3cm pompoms
- tracing paper, graphite paper & pencil
- white craft glue
- fine point permanent black marker
- paper towels

1. Glue medium box to top of large box and small box to top of medium box, centering each one side to side and matching up one side top to bottom for front edge.

2. Trace pattern for ears, paws and tail onto tracing paper, then use graphite paper to transfer patterns to heavy paper and cut out. Transfer kitten "chest" to front edge of box, matching top edge of chest to top edge of medium box lid.

3. Using round brush, paint paw pieces, tip of tail and chest white. Paint center of ears pink. Paint tail and remaining surfaces of boxes and ears in dark grey (insides of boxes can be painted dark grey as well). Allow paint to dry. Dip dry stencil brush in light grey paint, blot excess on paper towel, and gently dab brush over surface to create "fur" look.

4. Use graphite paper to transfer face to front of small box. With liner brush, paint eyes green, eye centers black with white

highlight, nose and mouth pink, and whiskers white. Outline around chest, eyes, nose, mouth and pink on ears with fine point marker.

5. Glue ears, paws, tail and pompoms in place on kitten.

$$ 6-10

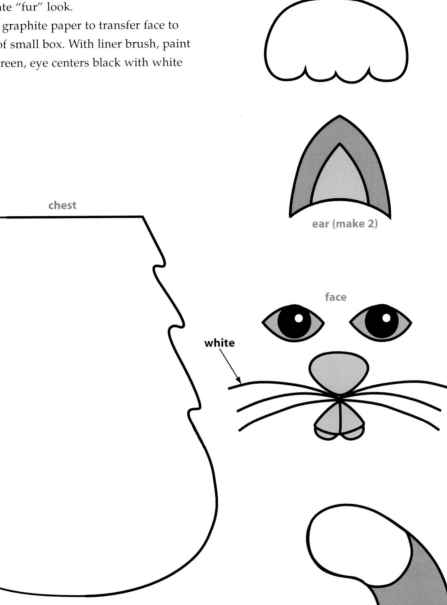

paw (make 2)

ear (make 2)

face

chest

white

tail

Nothing says home like a great big, comfy armchair. Pinpricked lines and a pinked border give this moving-day message the illusion of stitched fabric.

- medium-weight paper: one 12"/30.5cm square in ivory; one 6" x 8"/15cm x 20.5cm sheet in green; one 5" x 6"/12.5cm x15cm sheet in pink
- paper glue
- stylus & needles of different thicknesses
- tracing paper, graphite paper & pencil
- straight edge scissors & specialty scissors with contoured edges
- scrap of foam core board

Note: All piercing is done with needles, from either the front or back of the paper. The size of the needle used will determine the size of the pierced holes. Experiment with different combinations on scrap paper. Do all piercing on foam core board. This will provide a surface that will accept the needles and not mar your work surface. Use a stylus for embossing.

1. Cut an 8¾" x 11½"/22.5cm x 29.3cm rectangle from ivory paper. Fold rectangle in half to make card.

2. Trace patterns for card front, oval, doily and chair onto tracing paper. Place tracings over green, ivory and pink papers (refer to illustration for colors), and on back side of card front with graphite paper in between. Transfer patterns to papers.

3. For card front, cut side, open edge with specialty scissors. Pierce following curves of contoured edge. Emboss straight lines, then pierce between them.

4. Cut out oval using specialty scissors. Pierce following curves of contoured edge.

5. Pierce all lines on chair pattern closely together using a fine needle to give effect of solid line. Cut out chair approximately 1⁄16"/1.5mm outside of pierced lines using regular scissors. For doily, cut out top edge with regular scissors and sides and bottom with specialty scissors. Emboss straight lines, pierce between embossed lines as in border, then pierce in curves of contoured edges.

6. Center oval on card front and glue in place. Glue doily to top of chair, then glue chair over oval.

$ 1-5

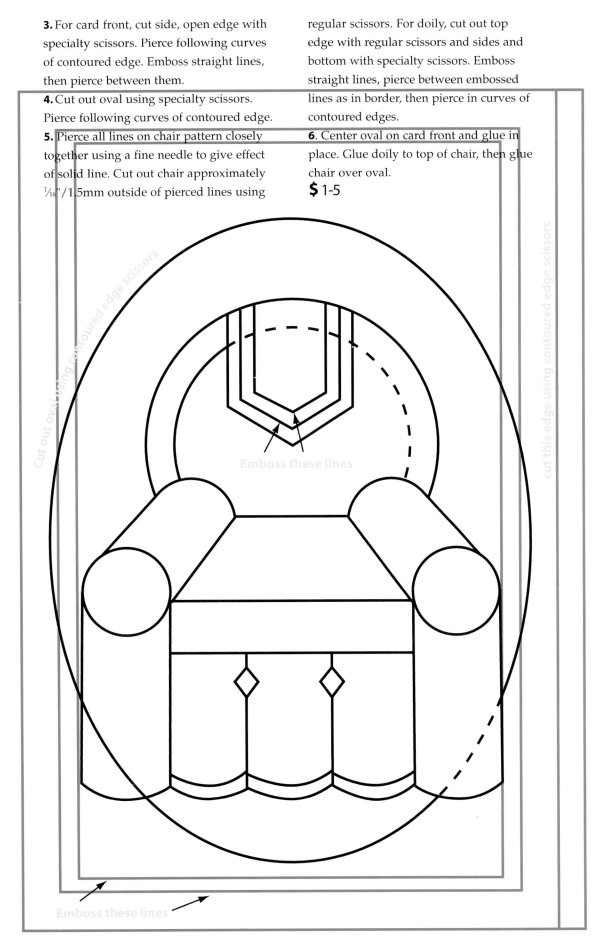

The months and days on this calendar can be changed so you will never be out of date. Instead of flowers, you can choose from an endless variety of motifs.

materials

- 1 sheet corrugated or other heavyweight paper, 19" x 23"/48.5cm x 58.5cm (lilac)
- 1 sheet heavyweight paper, 20" x 24"/51cm x 61cm (white)
- scraps or small sheets of textured paper for flowers & leaves: 10"/25.5cm square in pink; 4"/10cm square in purple; 3"/7.5cm square in light blue; 4"/10cm square in green
- paper glue
- photo corners
- tracing paper, pencil, ruler & graphite paper
- fine point markers: light blue, pink & green
- specialty scissors with contoured edges
- 17"/43cm twig for hanging

Note: The instructions call for one sheet of white paper. If you have small pieces of textured papers available, the decorative panel at the top can be done in one paper—as we have done—and the months and dates in another. Special dates, such as birthdays, anniversaries and holidays could also be cut out from other papers.

1. From corrugated paper, cut a 17" x 23"/43cm x 58.5cm piece for background, and two 4" x 1"/10cm x 2.5cm pieces for hanging loops. Cut a 8½" x 15"/21.8cm x 38cm piece for decorative panel, six 2" x 10½"/5cm x 26.8cm strips for months (use both sides), and forty-two 2" x 1½"/5cm x 3.8cm pieces for dates. Cut seven 1" x 2"/2.5cm x 5cm pieces for days of the week.

2. Trace patterns for flower, flower centers and leaves on tracing paper. Place tracings over colored papers with graphite paper in between. Transfer patterns to papers, then cut out. Leaves and flower centers can be cut out with specialty scissors. Glue centers to flowers, then glue flowers and leaves to decorative panel piece of paper.

3. Using colored markers, number all date pieces and write months on strips, one month on each side. Add letters to pieces for days of the week. Place photo corners on both lower corners of date pieces, day pieces, and month strips, and on all four corners of decorative panel. (For months that extend over five weeks, double number those squares in the fifth week, 23/30, 24/31 as an example.)

4. Working up from bottom of calendar, space date pieces approximately ⅜"/1cm apart, side to side and ⅜"/1cm up from bottom edge. Photo corners can be moistened (adhesive is already on back) and positioned in place. Repeat this all the way up for the remaining four weeks. Center month strip over dates side to side and ⅜"/1cm above dates. Center decorative panel piece in remaining space.

5. Fold 4" x 1"/10cm x 2.5cm pieces in half, gluing open ends to form loops. Glue loops to wrong side of calendar top, 2"/5cm in from each side. Place twig in loops for hanging.

$$ 6-10

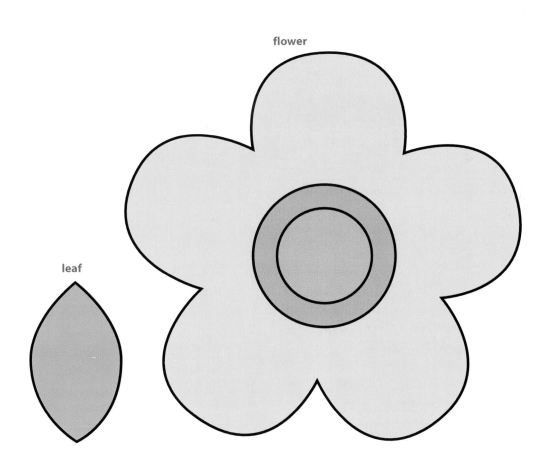

flower

leaf

paper platter

Make an attractive and durable storage tray by building up layers of corrugated cardboard on a glass or metal base.

- corrugated cardboard (recycle a box)
- découpage medium
- jute twine
- metal or glass loaf pan
- spongebrush
- white craft glue
- petroleum jelly & tack cloth
- bowl, water & paper towels

1. Apply a thin coat of petroleum jelly to inside of pan. (This will aid in releasing completed pan.) Tear cardboard into random pieces, not larger than 2" x 3"/5cm x 7.5cm. Place cardboard in bowl with some warm water. Soak for a few minutes until corrugated layers separate. Squeeze out excess water, then place between some paper towels to remove even more water.

2. Coat one side of paper with découpage medium and begin arranging paper inside pan, starting at bottom of pan and working up sides. Use fingers to smooth paper in place. Apply thin coat of medium over each layer of paper before applying next. Repeat process two more times so that there are three layers of paper. Wait until all three layers of paper are dry, 12 to 24 hours.

3. After paper "pan" is completely dry, carefully remove it from loaf pan. Wipe off any remaining petroleum jelly with a dry cloth. Add one or two more layers of paper on outside of paper "pan" to complete. (Paper can be kept in a plastic bag to remain moist.) Allow to dry completely, then apply another coat of découpage medium to inside and outside of "pan."

4. To make handles, knot three lengths of jute twine together, braid, and then knot opposite end. Make two braided handles, then glue one to each end of pan. Pan can be gently cleaned with a damp cloth.

$ 1-5

Thin strips of colored papers are woven to create a beautifully elegant note card perfect for any occasion.

materials

- 1 sheet medium-weight paper, 8½" x 11½"/21.8cm x 29.3cm
- 1 sheet medium-weight paper, 4¾" x 6½"/12cm x 16.3cm
- strips of paper in assorted colors: 4¾" x ¼"; 4¾" x ⅜"; 4¾" x ½"/12cm x 6mm; 12cm x 1cm; 12cm x 1.3cm
- paper glue, ruler, craft knife & pencil

Note: This card can be mailed in a standard 6" x 9"/15cm x 23cm clasp envelope.

1. Fold large sheet of paper in half crosswise to make card. Center and outline a 5½" x 3¾"/14cm x 9.5cm rectangle on card. Cut out to make window.

2. Leaving a ½"/1.3cm border on sides and top, use ruler and pencil to mark ½"/1.3cm vertical lines on small sheet of paper. With craft knife, cut along lines to make loom.

3. Weave strips of paper over and under cut out strips of loom. Alternate weaving pattern from row to row, lining up strips, leaving no gaps in between. Glue on ends of each strip to secure in place.

4. After all weaving is completed, glue woven sheet to back of card front, right side up and centered in window opening.

$ 1-5

Whether entertaining an intimate or large gathering, an elegant hand-decorated menu sets the stage for an unbeatable occasion.

- 15" x 12"/38cm x 30.5cm sheet medium-weight paper (natural)
- jute twine, wood beads & vinyl eraser
- acrylic paint: black & white
- alphabet stencil
- paintbrushes: round & stencil
- ruler, pencil & craft knife

1. On wrong side of paper, mark center of each long edge and draw line connecting marks. Fold paper in half and crease edge.

2. Open paper and lay flat on surface. Mark rectangle centered on right front half of cover. Divide rectangle into four even sections.

3. Cut eraser to size of section. With round brush, coat one side of eraser with black paint. Stamp black rectangle in bottom right and top left sections of rectangle. Let paint dry.

4. Stencil black "e" and "n" on appropriate white sections. Stencil white "m" and "u" on appropriate black sections. Let dry.

5. Fold in half. Cut length of twine long enough to wrap two and a half times around menu. Thread beads on twine and knot end to secure. Wrap twine around menu and slip beaded end under twine to hold in place.

$ 1-5

patchwork party bowl

A patchwork of brightly colored torn shapes makes a festive and sizzling design for a paper bowl. The finished bowl can be cleaned gently with a damp cloth.

materials

- medium-weight papers in assorted colors
- découpage medium
- four 20mm wood balls
- glass or other smooth surface bowl, approx. 6"/15cm diameter, 3"/7.5cm tall
- paintbrushes: sponge & round
- acrylic paint in coordinating color
- white craft glue
- petroleum jelly

1. Apply a thin coat of petroleum jelly to inside of bowl. (This will aid in releasing completed bowl.) Tear coloured papers into approximately 1"/2.5cm-wide strips, then tear strips into 1"/2.5cm squares. Paper will be arranged randomly in bowl.

2. Following manufacturer's guidelines, use spongebrush to coat one side of paper squares with découpage medium. Begin arranging rows of paper squares, angled and overlapping, starting at bottom of bowl and working up sides. Alternate colors for visual interest. Use fingers to smooth each paper square in place. If needed, apply thin coat of découpage medium over front side of paper pieces to keep them from lifting up or curling. As you reach top of bowl, angle paper pieces to create scalloped edge.

3. Allow first layer of paper to dry. Repeat process two more times so that there are three layers of paper. Let papers dry completely, then carefully remove paper "bowl" from glass bowl. Wipe off any remaining petroleum jelly with a dry cloth. Add another layer of paper squares on outside of "bowl" to finish. Allow to dry completely, then apply another coat of découpage medium to inside and outside of finished "bowl."

4. Using round brush, paint wood balls to coordinate with bowl. Glue balls to bottom of bowl. Let glue set.

$ 1-5

pillow panache

pillows are the most versatile of home furnishings. They provide color, pattern and design interest to a room and add softness and comfort to sofas and chairs.

Ordinary metal washers combine to make an extraordinary throw pillow to lend a stylish touch to a seating area.

materials

- two 16"/40.5cm squares of fabric
- 15"/38cm-square pillow form
- 13 small metal washers
- disappearing fabric marker
- sewing needle & matching thread
- sewing machine
- scissors

1. Beginning 3"/7.5cm from one edge, mark pillow top with five alternating rows of three and two washers, spacing rows 2½"/6.5cm apart. For rows of three, place a washer 3"/7.5cm in from each edge with a third spaced evenly between. For rows of two, center washers between first and second, and second and third washers of adjacent row.

2. Stitch washers to pillow top at markings. Insert needle from back side through center opening, stitch around one side of ring, then back through opening. Repeat to stitch on opposite side of ring. Continue stitching until all washers are in place.

3. Stitch pillow top and bottom right sides facing and edges aligned with ½"/1.3cm seam, leaving opening along one edge for turning and stuffing. Turn right side. Insert pillow form and slipstitch opening closed.

$ 1-5

table linen pillows

Elegant, vintage table linens are just too pretty to throw away. Making pillows is an easy way to give new life to old tablecloths.

materials

- old damask tablecloth
- 14"/35.5cm-square pillow form
- approx. 19"/48.5cm-square linen napkin
- 18"/46cm-square pillow form
- Battenberg doily
- crocheted doily
- fusible web or washable fabric glue
- sewing machine & matching thread
- scissors & straight pins

Note: Use leftover tablecloth fabric for back side of napkin pillow cover.

ruffled pillow

1. Cut tablecloth border into strips to make ruffles. Cut strips 6"/15cm wide and in longest lengths possible. Join strips by seaming short ends with ½"/1.3cm seam, until length of strip equals 112"/2.8m. Seam ends of strip to form circle, pressing all seams open. Fold circle in half lengthwise with right sides out and press.

2. Fold circle into four equal sections, using a pin to mark each fold. Make two rows of gathering stitches in each section beginning at fold and ending right before next fold. Pull up stitches to gather ruffle until circle fits perimeter of pillow.

3. Cut two 15"/38cm-square pieces from center of tablecloth for front and back of pillow cover.

4. Mark midpoint of each side of pillow front with pins. Match pins on ruffle to pins on pillow front. Pin ruffle on right side of pillow front with raw edges even. Make sure ruffles are spread evenly with a little extra fullness at the corners. Baste ruffle in place using ⅜"/1cm seam allowance. Remove pins.

5. With right sides together, pin pillow back to front, sandwiching ruffles. Stitch all around using ½"/1.3cm seam allowance, leaving an opening on one side for turning and stuffing. Remove pins, turn cover right side out and insert pillow form. Slipstitch opening closed.

napkin pillow

1. Following manufacturer's guidelines, apply fusible web to wrong side of Battenberg doily. Fuse doily in place at center of napkin. Doily could also be glued in place. Glue crocheted doily in place over Battenberg doily.

2. Cut a 19"/48.5cm square from leftover tablecloth fabric for back of napkin pillow. With right sides together and edges even, pin napkin to tablecloth square. Stitch all around using ½"/1.3cm seam allowance, leaving an opening on one side for turning and stuffing. Remove pins, turn right side out and insert pillow form. Slipstitch opening closed.

$ free

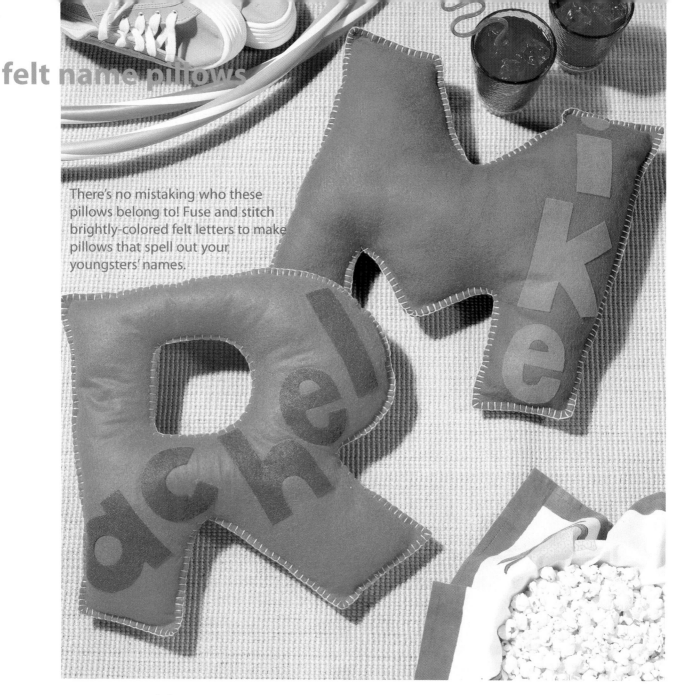

There's no mistaking who these pillows belong to! Fuse and stitch brightly-colored felt letters to make pillows that spell out your youngsters' names.

materials

- two 16"/40.5cm-square pieces of felt (for pillow front and back)
- 4"/10cm-square pieces of felt for small letters
- ¼yd/.25m paper-backed fusible web
- tracing paper & pencil
- 2 skeins 6-strand coordinating embroidery thread, #5 chenille needle, scissors & straight pins
- polyester fiberfill, iron & ironing board

Note: Cut pillow front and back (first letter of name) from one color and remaining letters from a contrasting color.

1. Outline a 16"/40.5cm square on tracing paper for first letter of name. (This will become the "pillow.") Outline a 4"/10cm square on tracing paper for each short letter in name and a 4" x 5"/10cm x 12.5cm rectangle for each tall letter. Outline letters freehand on tracing paper or trace letters from template provided. Letters should be as wide and high as possible. Pin tracing for first letter of name to large piece of felt and cut out two pieces.

2. Flip tracing paper for short and tall letters over to wrong side. Place fusible web over letters. Trace letters to paper side of web. Following manufacturer's guidelines, fuse letters to felt and cut out. Arrange smaller letters on front side of one large letter to spell out name. Fuse in place.

3. Pin large letters together, with name on front side and edges even. Using embroidery thread and needle, blanket-stitch all around letter (see diagram page 93), stuffing pillow with fiberfill as you go. For letters such as A, R, etc., blanket-stitch around opening in letter first, then around outside edges.

$ 1-5

uppercase letters: enlarge 200% four times
lowercase letters: enlarge 200% twice

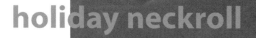

holiday neckroll

Deck your home for the holidays with a pretty roll pillow dressed up with poinsettia and winter greenery.

materials

Note: Use seasonal decorations to make pillows to suit different times of year.
- linen (or heavyweight cotton) dish towel
- fabric flowers & leaves
- cord or twine in coordinating color
- pillow form (see note below)
- all-purpose glue gun & glue sticks or fabric glue
- sewing machine & matching thread

Note: A pillow form can be made by tightly rolling batting (cut to width of pillow) into a roll. Glue ends of batting to secure.

1. If making a form, fold towel in half lengthwise with right sides facing. Using a ½"/1.3cm seam allowance, hand or machine stitch along long edge. If using a pillow form, measure circumference of form to determine finished circumference of roll, then add 1"/2.5cm for seam allowances. Trim towel to determined width. Fold in half lengthwise, right sides facing, and stitch along long edge with ½"/1.3cm seam. Turn right side out.

2. Place form inside roll, centering it side to side. Use cord to tie ends tightly against edge of form.

3. Glue leaves around cord, then glue small flower over leaves. Glue leaves to center of roll, then glue flowers in place.

$ 1-5

denim patchwork pillow

Nothing says comfort like an old pair of blue jeans. This patchwork pillow has a relaxed, laid-back style perfect for an outdoor patio or family room.

materials
- old denim jeans, jackets, shirts, etc.
- fabric scraps in coordinating colors/patterns
- 1yd/.95m paper-backed fusible web
- fabric scissors & pinking shears
- pencil & straight pins
- 18"/46cm-square pillow form
- iron & ironing board
- sewing machine & matching thread

1. Cut out nine 7"/18cm squares of denim for pillow front. Pillow back can be made by joining nine denim squares or by using one 19"/48.5 cm-square piece of fabric.
2. Outline smaller squares (1½", 2", 2½", 3", and 4"/3.8cm, 5cm, 6.5cm, 7.5cm and 10cm) on paper side of fusible web. Following manufacturer's guidelines, fuse squares to

fabric scraps and cut out using pinking shears. Fuse fabric squares to denim, overlapping and layering to create various quilt-like patterns.
3. Stitch denim squares to each other using ½"/1.3cm seam allowance. Stitch three squares together to form strips. Press seams open. Stitch three strips together to create pillow front. (If using denim squares for back, repeat process.)
4. Using ½"/1.3cm seam, stitch pillow front to back, right sides facing and edges even, leaving opening on one side for turning.
5. Turn right side out. Insert pillow form and slipstitch opening closed.
$ free

sheer beauty floral

Capture the beauty of a blooming summer garden with this breathtaking silk floral pillow cover.

- ½yd/.5m purple patterned fabric
- 11"/28cm-square piece of muslin
- 11"/28cm-square piece of white sheer fabric
- 15"/38cm-square piece of batting
- 1¾ yds/1.6m ⅛"/3mm-wide rope trim
- washable fabric glue & white craft glue
- gold beads
- 1 silk hydrangea stem
- 14"/35.5cm-square pillow form
- sewing needle
- scissors & straight pins
- iron & ironing board
- sewing machine & matching thread

1. Separate flowers and leaves from stem. Use fabric glue to tack leaves (should not be glued down completely) to muslin, centering leaves on fabric. Baste or carefully pin sheer fabric over muslin/leaves.

2. Cut two 11" x 3"/28cm x 7.5cm strips and two 15" x 3"/38cm x 7.5cm strips from patterned fabric and a 15"/38cm-square piece for pillow backing. With right sides facing, pin short strips to opposite sides of muslin. Stitch together using ½"/1.3cm seam allowance. Remove pins, and press seams open. Repeat with long strips on opposite sides.

3. Pin batting to wrong side of pillow top. Machine quilt around leaves. Zigzag stitch around edge of muslin.

4. With right sides together, pin pillow front to back. Stitch all around with ½"/1.3cm seam, leaving opening along one side for turning. Remove pins, turn right side out and insert pillow form. Slipstitch opening closed.

5. Use craft glue to glue rope trim around pillow edges, beginning at one corner and matching ends. Glue flowers to center of pillow top over leaves and one flower to each corner where fabrics meet. Glue beads to centers of flowers.

$$ 6-10

woven felt cushion

Pinked strips of felt in a soft blend of colors are woven together to create this clever and unique-looking throw pillow.

materials

- ½yd/.5m green felt
- 18" x 8"/46cm x 20.5cm piece of rose felt
- 18" x 8"/46cm x 20.5cm piece of vanilla felt
- 16"/40.5cm-square piece of fusible stabilizer
- rotary cutter with pinking blade & cutting mat
- 20"/51cm-square piece of corrugated cardboard
- straight pins, ruler & pencil
- iron, ironing board & pressing cloth
- 16"/40.5cm-square pillow form
- sewing machine & matching thread

1. Cut felt into strips using a rotary cutter and cutting mat. Cut eight 1" x

18"/2.5cm x 46cm strips of rose; eight 1" x 18"/2.5cm x 46cm strips of vanilla; eight 2" x 18"/5cm x 46cm strips and two 9 ½" x 18"/24.3cm x 46cm pieces of green.

2. Measure and mark an 18"/46cm square centered on cardboard. Using pins, anchor vertical strips of felt at top and bottom across width of marked square, referring to diagram for colors and placement (strips should be placed closed to the other). Repeat this process horizontally, anchoring all strips at one end and weaving over and under vertical strips. Slip stabilizer under felt with fusible side up, centering it under felt, then anchor free ends of horizontal strips.

3. Place pressing cloth over felt. Following manufacturer's instructions, fuse felt to stabilizer. Remove pins.

4. Turn woven felt over to wrong side. Pin larger pieces of green felt to woven felt, one piece on each side with pieces overlapping in center. Turn over to woven side.

5. Stitch all around using a straight or zigzag stitch, 1"/2.5cm in from edges. Trim edges even about ½"/1.3cm outside stitching lines. Slip pillow form through back opening.

$ 1-5

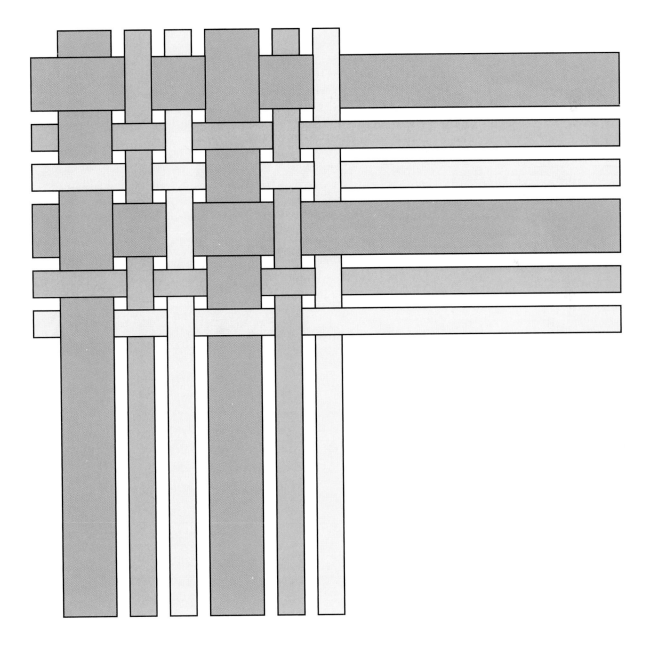

flower power pillows

Durable and soft terrycloth towels make the perfect fabric for a bright set of flower-shaped pillows. Toss a bunch on a floor, bed or chair to create a cozy corner.

- 1 bath towel (for flower)
- 1 hand towel or 2 washcloths in contrast color (for flower center)
- tracing paper & pencil
- scissors
- straight pins
- polyester fiberfill
- sewing machine & matching thread

1. Enlarge patterns (see opposite page) on photocopier to size of towels. Trace patterns for flower and center onto tracing paper. Pin patterns to towels and washcloths, cutting two flower shapes and two centers for front and back of pillow.

2. Fold edges of centers in ½"/1.3cm and pin one each to front and back of pillow. (Depending on type of towel you choose, there may be a side you prefer. Centers should be pinned to right sides.) Stitch centers to flowers ¼"/6mm in from edge. Remove pins.

3. With right sides facing, pin front and back of pillow together. Stitch all around with ½"/1.3cm seam, leaving opening for turning. Remove pins.

4. Clip seam allowances and curves and corners, then turn cover right side out.

5. Stuff pillow cover with fiberfill. Pin then slipstitch opening closed. Remove pins.

$ 1-5

enlarge to size of towels

sweet miss pillow

Delight young ones with this bright-eyed cutie, just right for cuddling up with.

materials

- ⅝yd/.6m muslin
- ½yd/.5m print fabric
- 1yd/.95m 1½"/3.8cm-wide lace
- 1yd/.95m ribbon, ⅝"/1.5cm wide
- ½yd/.5m ribbon, ⅛"/3mm wide
- 3 buttons & yarn
- white craft glue & washable fabric glue
- fabric paint: black, white & pink
- liner paintbrush
- 2 fabric daisies
- polyester fiberfill
- tracing paper & pencil
- dressmaker's carbon paper & stylus
- scissors & straight pins
- sewing machine & matching thread

1. Trace patterns for doll body (with facial features) and dress separately on tracing paper. Fold muslin and print fabric in half. Pin pattern for body to muslin and pattern for dress to print fabric. Use dressmaker's carbon and stylus to transfer facial features to muslin. Cut out two pieces each for doll body and dress (facial features will be on only one muslin piece).

2. Use fabric glue to glue dress pieces to muslin. Apply glue to cuffs, neck and randomly on remainder of dress. (This will hold dress to body while you are adding embellishments.) On both dress pieces, glue strips of lace to cuffs and neck. Glue ribbon to cuffs, just covering edges of lace. Let glue dry.

3. Paint facial features with liner brush. Paint nose black, mouth and cheeks pink, and eyes white with black details. Let dry.

4. Cut two strips of lace equal to length of lower dress hem. With right sides facing, match edge of lace to raw edge of dress hem and pin. Repeat for other piece. Place right sides of pillow front and back together and pin. Stitch all around with ½"/1.3cm seam, leaving an opening along one side. Remove pins, clip curved seams, and turn pillow right side out. Stuff firmly,

then slipstitch opening closed.

5. Cut thirty 3"/7.5cm lengths of yarn and forty five 27"/68.5cm lengths. Use craft glue to glue 3"/7.5cm lengths (bangs) one next to the other, starting at center top of head at seam line, and working out to both sides of head. Trim evenly. Starting at top of head, overlap first two or three 27"/68.5cm lengths of yarn over top edge of bangs. Continue gluing on yarn, working to back of head, centering lengths down back. Allow glue to dry. Pull yarn together at each side of head and braid. Tie each braid with a piece of narrow ribbon. Trim ends. Glue daisy to ribbon on each braid.

6. Glue buttons to front of dress. Tie bow with remaining length of wide ribbon and glue to front center at neck.

$$ 6-10

roped pillow

Swirl and criss-cross twine and glue in place to add texture and decorative interest to a plain pillow top.

materials

- plain pillow, approx. 16"/40.5cm square
- jute twine
- all-purpose glue gun & glue sticks or white craft glue
- 5" x 3"/12.5cm x 7.5cm piece of heavy cardboard
- scissors

1. Lay twine out on surface of pillow. Surface can be divided into grid with a design in each section, or surface can be decorated with overall design. Glue rope decorations in place on pillow.

2. To make each tassel, wrap twine around cardboard (5"/12.5cm width) six times.

Cut a 14"/35.5cm length of twine and slip one end through one end of wrapped twine. Tie tightly, then use scissors to open loops at other end. Remove cardboard. Take another length of twine (approximately 12"/30.5cm) and wrap five or six times around tassel about ½"/1.3cm down from top. Knot ends to secure. Twine can be untwisted to create fuller tassel. Repeat to make four tassels.

3. Glue a tassel to each pillow corner, looping ends of twine at top of tassel and gluing in place as shown.

$ 1-5

Make an ordinary flanged pillow even more special by transferring on a favorite photo or print.

materials
- ½yd/.95m muslin
- photo and print & transfer medium
- 12"/30.5cm-square pillow form
- needle, scissors & straight pins
- sewing machine & matching thread
- iron & ironing board

1. Cut two 17"/43cm-squares from muslin for pillow front and back.

2. Follow manufacturer's instructions to transfer photo/print to center of one muslin square for pillow front.

3. Pin pillow front to back, right sides facing and edges even. Stitch with ½"/1.3cm seam, leaving 12"/30.5cm opening along one side for stuffing. Turn right side out and press.

4. Topstitch all around 2"/5cm from edge, beginning and ending at opening.

5. Insert pillow form through opening.

6. Topstitch pillow area closed with zipper foot, starting and ending at stitching line. Slipstitch flange opening closed.

$$ 6-10

green basketweave pillow

A pretty basketweave pattern knit in a cool, cotton blend gives this pillow glowing color and texture.

materials

- two 1³⁄₄oz/50g balls sport-weight yarn in lime
- one pair size 3 (3mm) needles OR SIZE TO OBTAIN GAUGE
- for fabric backing: 16"/43cm-square piece of fabric
- 15"/38cm-square pillow form
- 8 lime-colored buttons
- sewing needle & scissors
- sewing machine & matching thread

gauge

20 sts and 32 rows to 4"/10cm over basketweave pattern. Size: pillow is 16"/40cm square.

TAKE TIME TO CHECK GAUGE

Note: Yarn amounts given are enough to make pillow front. If knitting the back, adjust yarn amounts accordingly.

basketweave pattern

(multiple of 8 sts)

Rows 1 and 3 (RS) *K4, p4; rep from * to end.

Rows 2 and all WS rows K the knit sts and p the purl sts.
Rows 5 and 7 *P4, k4; rep from *.
Rows 6 and 8 K4, p4; rep from *.
Rep rows 1-8 for basketweave pat.

pillow

Cast on 80 sts. Work in basketweave pat for 16"/40cm. Bind off in pat.

finishing

Block pieces to measurements. Place knit cover and fabric backing right sides together, and machine-stitch along three sides with ½"/1.3cm seam allowance. Turn right side out, and insert pillow form. Sew remaining side closed. Measure 4½"/11.5cm in from each edge to form 7"/18cm square in center of pillow top. Mark corners of square with thread. Stitch first button at marking, going through pillow, and out through second button in corresponding position on pillow bottom. Continue stitching until buttons are secured in placed. Repeat to stitch buttons on each corner of marked square.

$$ 6-10

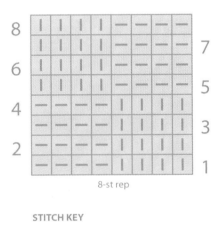

8-st rep

STITCH KEY

K on RS, p on WS

P on RS, k on WS

Knit Abbreviations:
approx—approximately; k—knit; p—purl; pat(s)—pattern(s); rep—repeat; RS—right side; st(s)—stitch(es); WS—wrong side.

ottoman footstool

Put your feet up and relax with this lovely, overstuffed footstool made from a recycled, jumbo-sized popcorn tin.

materials

- large tin, approx 10"/25.5cm diameter, 12"/30.5cm tall (from popcorn, pretzels, etc.)
- ½yd/.5m fabric, 4.5yds/4.15m wide (for skirt)
- 18"/46cm-square piece of fabric (for top)
- 1yd/.95m fringe trim, 2½"/6.5cm wide
- 12"/30.5cm-square pillow form or 12"/30.5cm-diameter form
- 2 buttons, approx. 1"/2.5cm diameter
- sewing needle
- iron & ironing board
- button, carpet thread & long needle
- all-purpose glue gun & glue sticks
- sewing machine & matching thread

1. Cut fabric for skirt 2½"/6.5cm longer than height of can. Seam side ends right sides together with ½"/1.3cm seam to make one continuous fabric loop. Press seams open. Fold and press bottom hem ½"/1.3cm, then ½"/1.3cm again and edgestitch. Stitch two rows of basting stitches, using loose tension and heavier bobbin thread, ½"/1.3cm and ¼"/6mm from top fabric edge. Pull bobbin thread to gather fabric. Remove top from can and slip skirt over can, adjusting gathers evenly to fit around can. Stitch to secure gathers. Fold gathered edge over top edge of can and glue in place, being sure that skirt reaches bottom of can.

2. Center fabric for footstool top over pillow form and center one button on fabric. Thread needle and leaving a 4"/10cm length of thread at top, take a stitch straight down through button and pillow form and through second button. Come back up through second button, through pillow and up through first button. Repeat to secure buttons. (If desired, use a double length of thread.) Tie ends of thread securely, tufting the pillow.

3. Turn can lid upside down. Glue bottom of pillow to inside of lid. Scrunch pillow form to fit inside lid. Bring edge of fabric around to top of lid, pulling fabric taut to smooth, and glue in place on lid top.

4. Glue tufted lid to skirted can bottom. Glue trim around footstool, covering seam where lid and bottom fabrics meet.

$$ 6-10

speedy stitchery

i t's the details that really make a difference. In this chapter, you will find a variety of special, yet simple-to-sew projects that take less than a day to accomplish.

A pretty ceramic teacup makes a lovely base for a pincushion. With coordinating fabric and trim, it makes a nice table decoration.

materials

- ceramic teacup
- approx. 10"/25.5cm-square piece of coordinating fabric
- polyester fiberfill
- needle & matching thread
- all-purpose glue gun & glue sticks
- ⅛"/3mm-wide cord trim
- embroidery scissors

Note: Material amounts will vary depending on the size of the teacup used.

1. Cut a piece of fabric 3"/7.5cm larger all around than diameter of teacup top.

2. Thread needle and sew all around with running stitch ⅜"/1cm from edge of fabric, gently gathering as you stitch. Stuff cushion with fiberfill until firm. Pull gathers tightly and knot ends of thread to secure.

3. Apply glue to inside edge of cup. Push cushion down into cup. Loop remaining trim through handle and tie to scissors.

4. Glue trim around base of cup and around top edge of cup around cushion.

$ free

cupcake wall hanging

materials

- 2 fabric napkins, approx. 17"/43cm square
- felt: 4" x 7"/10cm x 18cm piece each of pink, white, brown & yellow (for icings); four 9" x 12"/23cm x 30.5cm pieces of peach (for cakes)
- 1yd/.95m 1"/2.5cm-wide ribbon
- four 1"/2.5cm red buttons
- ½yd/.5m quilt batting
- ½yd/.5m paper-backed fusible web
- ½yd/.5m cord & 18"/46cm-long twig
- white craft glue
- assorted colors of acrylic paint
- toothpicks

- air soluble fabric marking pen
- iron & ironing board
- pencil & tracing paper
- straight pins & scissors
- sewing machine

1. Cut length of ribbon in half. Following manufacturer's guidelines, fuse web to wrong side of both pieces. Remove paper and fuse ribbons, one vertical and one horizontal, to one napkin, dividing it into four equal sections for front of hanging.

2. Trace patterns and all pattern markings for icing and cake onto paper side of fusible web. Repeat to make four cake and four icing pieces. Fuse web to felt and cut out shapes. With fabric marker, mark stitching lines ¼"/6mm in from edges of cake pieces.

3. For each piece of felt (four icings, four cakes), cut a piece of batting ¼"/6mm smaller all around. Place batting for cakes on front of hanging, one in each section. Remove paper backings, center felt pieces over batting and fuse. Topstitch along marked lines. Place batting for icings in place over cakes. Remove paper backings, center felt pieces over batting and fuse.

4. Cut a piece of batting ¼"/6mm smaller all around than size of napkin. Lay undecorated napkin on flat surface and center batting, then front of hanging, face up on top. Baste or carefully pin all three layers together. Machine-stitch along either side of vertical and horizontal ribbon strips, then stitch around edges of napkin using either a straight or zigzag stitch. Remove basting stitches/pins.

5. Glue buttons to the top of each cupcake. Dip toothpick (using a separate one for each color) into paint, and paint small dots on top of cupcakes for sprinkles.

6. Cut cord into three equal pieces. Knot ends together to form three loops. Stitch or glue loops to back of hanging at top edge, one on each side and one in the middle. Slip twig through loops for hanging.

$$ 6-10

icing

placement line for icing

cake

tablecloth place mats

Cut out the "good" parts of a stained or partially worn tablecloth to make a nice set of place mats. Large napkins in coordinating colors can also be used.

**materials
to make four place mats**

- tablecloth
- 1yd/.95m fabric for backing (If there is enough fabric left, tablecloth fabric can be used for backing. If not, select a fabric that coordinates, but has a different look so place mats can be reversible.)
- 1yd/.95m low-loft quilt batting
- scissors, ruler, straight pins & iron

1. For each place mat, cut a piece of tablecloth, backing fabric and quilt batting, each 13" x 17"/33cm x 43cm (this includes ½"/1.3cm seam allowance all around).

2. For each place mat, lay a piece of batting on a flat surface. Lay tablecloth fabric right side up over batting, and backing fabric wrong side up over tablecloth fabric. Pin layers together.

3. Stitch all around, leaving an opening along one side for turning. Turn right sides out and press seams flat, turning under open edges. Pin around edges to keep smooth. Topstitch all around about ¼"/6mm in from edge to close opening and add a nice finish.

$ 1-5

Pretty quilted squares turn functional pot holders into customized decorative accents for your kitchen.

**materials
to make 2 pot holders**
• two 9"/23cm quilt squares (recycled from an old quilt)
• two 9"/23cm squares of fabric
• two 9"/23cm squares of batting
• 1 package extra-wide double-fold bias tape
• straight pins, needle & matching thread
• sewing machine

1. For each pot holder, place fabric square wrong-side-up on flat surface. Layer square of batting over fabric and quilt square right-side-up over batting. Pin then baste layers together, running basting stitches corner to corner and across center in both directions. Remove pins.

2. Machine or hand quilt. Quilting can be done along seam lines or in a pattern of your choice.

3. Double-fold bias tape is folded with one side wider than the other. Pin bias tape to edges of pot holder with wider side underneath, facing fabric. (This will ensure that all three layers are caught when stitching.) Leave 4"/10cm of bias tape at one corner of pot holder for loop. Fold loop in half, insert end between edges of binding. Sew along binding edges and across base of loop to secure in place.

$ 1-5

striped tea cozy

Cold tea in the pot? This p[...]y will add a splash of color an[...] pattern [...] kitchen while keeping [...] nice and warm.

materials

- ⅜yd/.35m lightweight cotton fabric
- single-fold bias tape in coordinating colors: 2 packages each in light blue & medium blue; 1 package each in dark blue & very dark blue
- ⅜yd/.35m batting
- ½yd/.5m fusible web
- ½yd/.95m ⅛"/3mm-wide rope trim
- tracing paper & pencil
- scissors & straight pins
- needle & matching thread
- sewing machine
- fabric glue
- iron & ironing board
- tassle

1. Enlarge pattern to size on a photocopier. Trace pattern for base/backing onto tracing paper and cut out. Pin pattern to fabric and cut out two base and two backing pieces. Use same pattern to cut two pieces of batting. Cut fusible web into strips with same width as bias tape.

2. Place base pieces on ironing board. Cut strips of bias tape 2"/5cm longer than width of base pieces. Following manufacturer's guidelines, fuse web strips to wrong side of bias tape. Arrange horizontal strips of bias tape side by side on base pieces until entire surface is covered with striped pattern. Remove paper backing from web and fuse bias tape strips in place, starting at the bottom edge of first base piece. Repeat this process for second base piece.

3. Place a piece of batting on your work surface. Lay a backing piece right-side-up over batting, then striped base piece right-side-down over backing. Pin or baste all three layers together securely so they will remain smooth when sewing. Sew all three layers together with ½"/1.3cm seam, leaving opening at bottom for turning. Turn right sides out and slipstitch opening closed. Repeat for second base piece.

4. Steam edges flat. With wrong sides facing, pin front and back pieces together with tassle in between. Machine-stitch front to back approximately ¼"/6mm in from outside edge and flip right sides out. Glue rope trim between front and back pieces, in channel created when sewing front and back pieces together.

$$ 6-10

pattern for base and backing
enlarge 177%

fabric gift bags

While bottles of wine and jars of jam make pleasurable gifts, their odd shapes make them hard to wrap. These fabric bags are a great gift-wrapping solution.

materials

- sheer fabrics
- ribbon for ties
- tape measure & scissors
- sewing machine & matching thread
- iron

1. Measure width of bottle/jar and add 2"/5cm. Measure height of bottle/jar. Double height measurement, then add width measurement plus 4"/10cm. Cut fabric to these dimensions.

2. Fold fabric in half crosswise with right sides facing. Stitch sides together using ½"/1.3cm seam allowance. Turn right side out.

3. If hemming top edge, fold and press hem ¼"/6mm, then ¼"/6mm again and stitch in place. Slip gift in bag and tie on top with a coordinating ribbon.

4. If making a casing for top edge (for drawstring), press under ¼"/6mm, then ¾"/2cm. Stitch close to inside fold, stitching and then backstitching over one of the side seams. Stitch again close to outside fold. With scissors blade, split side seam open lengthwise (on side that was backstitched) between rows of stitching. Weave ribbon through casing, then tie ribbon in bow to close.

$ 1-5

lush velvet scarf

This luxurious velvet scarf is surprisingly quick and easy to make. It's perfect for a night out or to add a hint of glamour to your everyday wardrobe.

materials

- ¼yd/.25m velvet (approx. 54"/137cm wide)
- ¼yd/.25m lining fabric (same width as velvet)
- ½yd/.5m fringe
- scissors & straight pins
- sewing machine & matching thread

1. If necessary, trim velvet and lining fabric to exactly the same size.

2. Place velvet and lining right sides facing and edges even. Cut trim in half. Place trim between velvet and lining at each end with raw edges even and fringe facing in. Pin layers together.

3. Stitch all around with ½"/1.3cm seam, leaving an opening along one side for turning. Remove pins and turn right side out. Fold under raw edges and pin opening closed. Smooth scarf, then topstitch all around ¼"/6mm in from edges to finish. Remove pins.

$$ 6-10

Keep little ones toasty warm with a cute and comfy mittens and scarf set. They're a breeze to make from snuggly-soft polar fleece.

- ½yd/.5m polar fleece
- 2 skeins contrasting embroidery floss
- ruler, tracing paper & pencil
- tape measure
- embroidery needle
- scissors & straight pins
- sewing machine & matching thread

Note: There is no wrong side to polar fleece, but all pieces should be cut in the same direction as fabric stretches differently in either direction.

1. Cut a 10" x 45"/25.5cm x 114.5cm piece of fleece for the scarf. Round off corners. Thread embroidery needle with embroidery thread and blanket-stitch around edges (see diagram, opposite page).

2. To make pattern for mittens, place child's hand on tracing paper with thumb positioned at about a 45° angle from other fingers, and other fingers slightly separated. Outline hand, starting at one side of wrist and ending at other side. Smooth lines to look like mitten. Draw a straight line across wrist. Add ½"/1.3cm seam allowance all around and cut out. For cuff pattern, measure width of wrist, add 1"/2.5cm for seams and cut rectangle from tracing paper this width by 3"/7.5cm. Use patterns to cut out two cuff and two hand pieces for each mitten.

3. Pin two hand pieces together and sew all around with ½"/1.3cm seam allowance, leaving bottom edge (wrist) open. Sew two cuff pieces together at each side end, right sides facing with ½"/1.3cm seam. Trim seams and turn both pieces right sides out.

4. Slip cuff inside mitten, so right side of cuff is against wrong side of mitten and top edges are matching. Pin in place, then sew together with ½"/1.3cm seam allowance. Trim seams, pull cuff out and fold over right side of mitten. Blanket-stitch around bottom edge of cuff.

$ 1-5

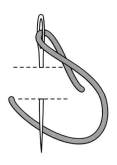
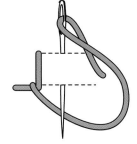
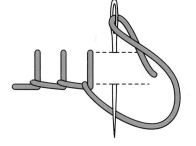

blanket stitch

ribbon organizer

In place of a run-of-the-mill bulletin board, make this good-looking organizer to store notes, cards and more.

materials
- frame with cardboard backing
- assorted ribbons in complementary colors, 1"/2.5cm to 2½"/6.5cm wide
- white fabric remnant
- white acrylic paint & wash paintbrush
- sewing machine & thread
- scissors & straight pins
- white craft glue

1. Remove backing from frame. Paint frame white and let dry.

2. Cut fabric 2"/5cm larger than backing all around. Cut strips of ribbon to length equal to width of backing plus 2"/5cm. Lay strips horizontally over fabric, overlapping layers to form pockets. Pin ribbon strips in place.

3. Stitch along lower edges and ends of ribbons to secure to fabric. (Double-up narrower ribbons and stitch only along bottom edge of lower ribbon to form pocket.)

4. Place ribboned cloth face up over cardboard backing. Fold edges to back side and glue in place. Place backing in frame and hang.

$ 1-5

An outdoor tablecloth is reborn as a bright smock for your child. The durable plastic surface allows paint spills to wipe up easily.

materials
- plastic tablecloth & double fold bias binding
- pinking shears, straight pins, & white craft glue
- large sheet of paper & pencil

1. To make the smock pattern, draw a straight line along one edge of tracing paper. Place paper on floor and have child lie face-up on it with his/her arms out perpendicular to their body, just under drawn line. Draw line parallel to the one drawn, running 6"/15cm below undersides of arms. Draw lines running 6"/15cm out and along each side of child's body and a connecting line at each wrist. Mark length (hip, knee or any length in between). Mark neck 2"/5cm out from each side of child's neck.

2. Left and right sides of pattern should mirror, and all lines should be either parallel or perpendicular. Adjust pattern as needed. Outline neck with a curve from side to side.

3. Pin pattern to tablecloth. Using pinking shears, cut out two pieces. Cut two 6" x 8"/15cm x 20.5cm pocket pieces (or larger).

4. Fold under edges ¼"/6mm and topstitch pockets to front of smock along three sides, leaving top open. With right sides facing, pin front and back of smock together. Stitch around sides, undersides and tops of sleeves with ½"/1.3cm seam allowance. Use pinking shears to cut back in half right down center. Remove pins and turn right side out.

5. Center 1yd/.95m length of binding at center of neck front and glue or stitch in place around neck, leaving long trailing ends at back. Topstitch ends along open edge to make ties.

$ 1-5

embroidered-daisy pillows

Liven up a seating area with a jumble of brightly-colored throw pillows adorned with a garden of embroidered daisies.

- two 17"/43cm-square pieces of fabric
- 16"/40.5cm-square pillow form
- 71"/180cm strip of double-fold bias binding
- 71"/180cm length of cotton cord
- 12 embroidered daisy appliqués
- tape measure & fabric marker
- scissors & straight pins
- sewing machine & matching thread
- iron & ironing board
- small plate
- fabric glue

1. Open bias tape and press flat. Place cord along center of tape. Fold tape around cord with edges even and pin. Using zipper foot, machine-stitch layers together close to cording (without stitching into it) to make piping.

2. Trace around plate to round corners of fabric squares. Cut along markings. Measure and mark right side of pillow top piece with three evenly-spaced rows of four daisies. Follow manufacturer's instructions to apply glue to back of daisy. Adhere daisy to pillow at marking. Repeat to adhere remaining daisies.

3. Pin piping to right side of pillow top piece, matching raw edges. Place pins closer together at corners, easing piping around curves and clipping seam allowance at intervals to make piping lay flat. Pin ends right sides facing, fitting strip to pillow. Stitch ends together and trim seam allowance.

4. Pin both pillow pieces together, right sides facing. Sew close to cord, leaving opening along one edge for turning. Turn right side out, insert pillow form and slipstitch opening closed.

$$ 6-10

cross-stitch pillow

Beautiful for Christmas or any time of year,
this sumptuous velvet pillow is adorned
with a charming cross-stitch of a holly leaf
surrounded by red berries.

materials

- 10"/25.5cm square 10-count waste canvas
- DMC embroidery floss, one skein of each color listed in key, opposite page
- #18 tapestry & #10 embroidery needle
- one 14"/35.5cm square each of yellow ochre velvet & cotton fabric
- 14"/35cm-square pillow form
- scissors, straight pins & ruler
- terrycloth towel & press cloth
- iron & ironing board
- sewing machine & matching thread
- spray water bottle & tweezers

pillow is 12"/30cm square
cross-stitch is 5"/12cm square

1. Fold canvas cloth in quarters to determine center. Mark center with basting lines lengthwise and widthwise. Baste waste canvas to center of pillow top.

2. Starting in center of cloth, follow chart to cross-stitch motifs, using three strands of floss in needle. (Symbols on chart refer to colors in color key.) When working cross-stitch, make sure upper half of all crosses lay in same direction. When motifs are completed, cross-stitch background using two strands of white and one strand of yellow #3819 held together. Fill in back-

background until cross-stitch measures 5"/12.5cm square. Satin stitch (see diagram below) around edges with background thread over 3 threads of canvas. Place finished piece face down on terrycloth towel, cover with damp press cloth and press. Trim canvas, leaving ¼"/6mm border around cross-stitch.

3. Following manufacturers instructions, spray cross-stitch with water until damp. Using tweezers, gently remove canvas threads, one thread at a time.

4. Pin pillow top and bottom pieces right sides facing and edges even. Stitch all around with ½"/1.3cm seam, leaving opening on one edge for turning. Turn right side out, insert pillow form, and slipstitch opening closed.

$$ 6-10

color key

- ⊡ white
- ○ pale peach—DMC 3825
- ⊠ dark peach—DMC 3340
- ■ medium red—DMC 350
- ■ dark red—DMC 347
- ⧗ dark brown—DMC 801
- ▲ medium taupe—DMC 3782
- V pale green—DMC 368
- V medium green—DMC 320
- ⧄ medium/dark green—DMC 367
- ● dark green—DMC 319
- △ golden yellow—DMC 725

background color:
hold together 2 strands whiteand one strand yellow—DMC 3819

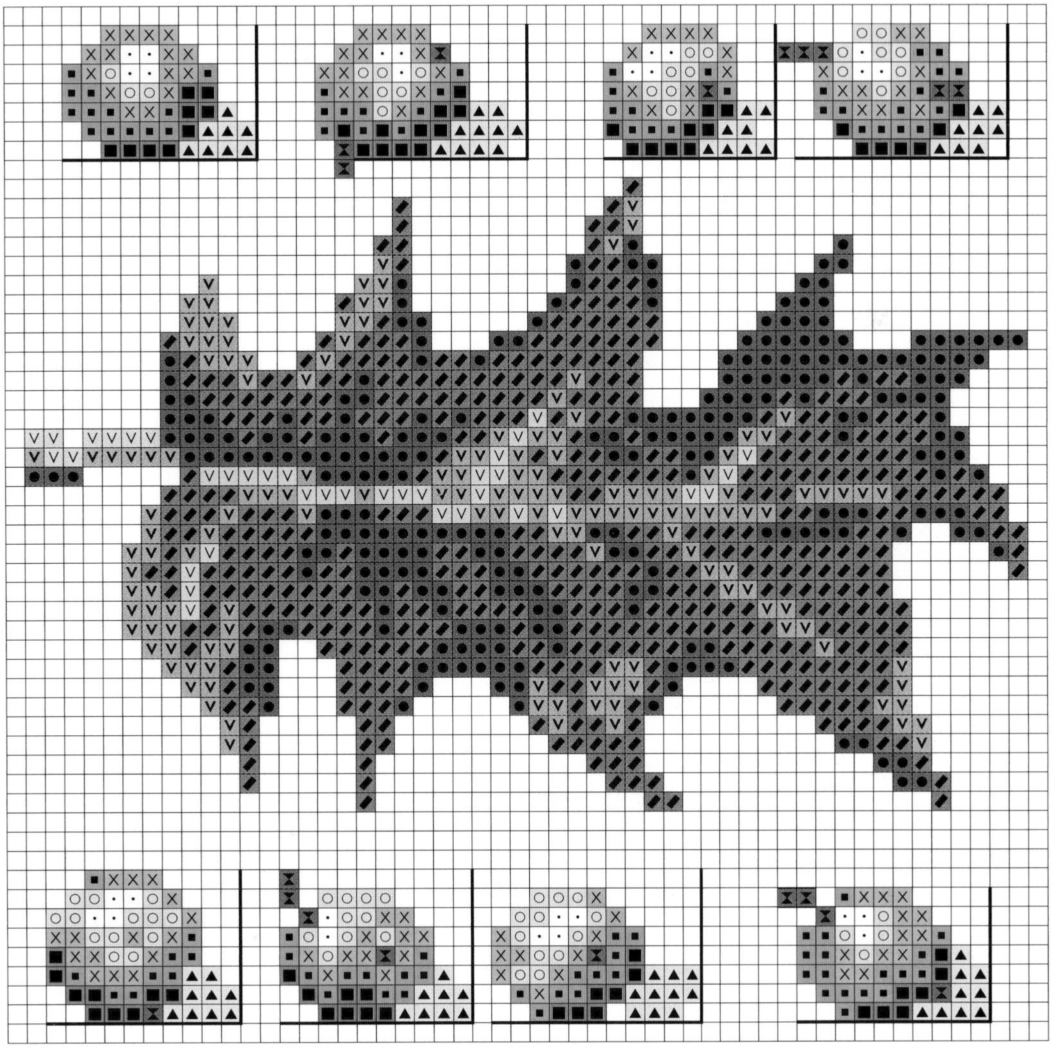

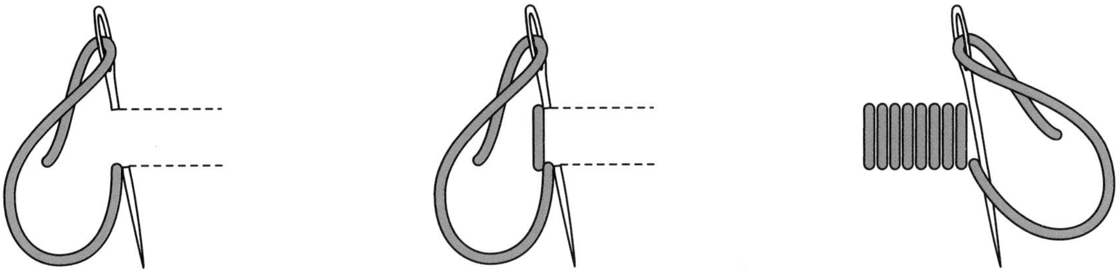

satin stitch

With each season, nature offers a fresh bounty of
creative inspiration. A walk in the woods or a
stroll on the beach can reveal all the raw materials
needed to create lovely accents for your home.

Don't let your favorite blooms fade from memory! Press them into delicate, two-dimensional decorations perfect for embellishing painted storage boxes.

materials

- found wooden box
- light blue acrylic paint & fine sandpaper
- découpage medium
- pressed flowers & foliage
- paintbrushes: wash & sponge
- tweezers & cotton swab
- disposable dish

1. With wash, paint box with two coats blue paint. Let dry, then lightly sand to reveal base.

2. Dry flowers with purchased flower-press or hand-press flowers between sheets of absorbent paper weighted with heavy book. Plan placement of pressed flowers before gluing.

3. Pour découpage medium into dish. Carefully hold dried flower with tweezers. Using brush or cotton swab, gently dab medium on back of petals.

4. Position and glue flower on box top. Gently press in place and smooth with cotton swab. Repeat to glue remaining flowers and leaves to box.

5. With spongebrush, carefully apply layer of medium over flowers and leaves. Use tweezers to reposition any broken petals and glue in place. Wait about 10 minutes for glue to dry. Apply several coats of medium over surface of box top. Let dry.

$ free

Make attractive mini houses coated with peanut butter and seeds to decorate your yard and delight your feathered friends.

materials

- cardboard milk carton (quart or half gallon)
- scrap pieces of wood (slightly larger than base of milk carton)
- peanut butter & craft stick
- birdseed, sheet moss, pinecones, dried corn husks (from tops of Indian corn) & jute twine
- all-purpose glue gun & glue sticks
- glass, pencil & craft knife
- 8"/20.5cm piece of 14 gauge wire (or piece from wire hanger)
- wax paper
- scissors & wire cutter (optional)

Note: Be sure to hang the feeders out of reach of cats and other predators.

1. Rinse out milk carton and allow to dry thoroughly. Glue pouring spout closed. Pierce a hole at top center of carton for hanger. Bend wire to form hook or twist to form loop. Insert wire in hole on top of house.

2. Use a glass or small bowl as a template for the birdhouse "door." Cut out opening with craft knife.

3. With stick, coat all four sides of carton with thin layer of peanut butter. Spread birdseed out on sheet of waxed paper. Press coated sides of container into seeds until peanut butter is covered.

4. Glue sheet moss to bottom of wood scrap. Center carton on top of wood scrap and glue in place. Glue moss around house on top and sides of wood.

5. To make "thatched" roof, glue pieces of husk along top edge of container. If husks stand away from container, add glue along sloped edge of container to secure. Trim husk edges even. To make "shingle" roof, use scissors or wire cutter to clip petals from pinecones as close to center of cone

as possible. Begin by gluing petals, one right next to the other along bottom edge of sloped part of container. Glue next row overlapping the first so that only tips of previous row are exposed. Continue until entire roof is covered.

6. Wipe peanut butter and seeds from around door opening. Glue pinecone petals or braided jute twine around door (knot ends of twine before applying). Hang from sturdy branch.

$ 1-5

twig
cap rack

No matter how limited you consider your woodworking skills to be, you can easily make this handsome and handy hat rack.

materials
- twigs: two 24"/61cm long, ½"/1.3cm diameter; five 14"/35.5cm long, ½"/1.3cm diameter; eight 2½"/6.5cm long, ¼"/6mm diameter
- chisel (½"/1.3cm wide), coping saw & drill
- wood glue, wire nails, hammer & pencil

1. Using saw, cut all twigs to sizes indicated. Arrange twigs to form rack. Place horizontal twigs (24"/61cm) down first, then vertical (14"/35.5cm) twigs. Leave 2"/5cm at each end (vertical and horizontal) for border. Space vertical twigs evenly within borders.

2. Mark each intersection with two lines, one on each side. At markings, use saw to cut notches halfway through twig. Cut through top half of horizontal twigs and through bottom half of vertical twigs.

3. Use chisel to carve wood from between notches to about half of twig diameter. Fit vertical and horizontal twigs together. If needed, adjust size and depth of notches so twigs lay flat.

4. Apply glue to notches and join pieces. Secure joined pieces at intersections by nailing through back side.

5. Use drill bit about same size as pegs (2½"/6.5cm pieces). Drill holes, angled 45° up, between each vertical twig, about halfway through twig. Apply glue in each hole and insert pegs.

$ free

A stroll through the woods—or even your backyard—is all that's needed to gather the materials for these stunning containers. Group several on a desktop or table.

materials

- small papier-mâché boxes (approx. 3"/7.5cm square, 3"/7.5cm diameter, 4"/10cm oval)
- pinecones, small twigs & watermelon seeds
- pruning shears
- white craft glue & waterbased protective finish
- wash paintbrush & pencil
- optional: acrylic paint in black or dark brown

1. Paint boxes or leave their natural color. Allow all natural materials to dry before applying to boxes.

2. Place lid on box and lightly pencil mark line around bottom of lid lip. Do not glue materials above this line or lid will not fit.

3. Glue watermelon seeds one next to another in rows around box and box lid.

For top of lid, begin by gluing seeds around outside edge and work inward.

4. Clip "petals" from pinecones with pruning shears. Starting at bottom of box, glue rows of "petals" around box and box lid, with "petal" tips overlapping "petal" bases of each previous row. For top of lid, begin by gluing "petals" to outside edge and work inward.

5. Clip twigs to uniform lengths to fit around bottom of box and box lid. Top of box can be done in one direction or divided into sections with twigs cut to fit.

6. Complete each box by brushing on a coat of protective finish.

$ 1-5

floral fantasy lamp

Sunny yellow fabric and rings of glorious daisies turn a once plain-Jane lamp into a flowering decorative showpiece.

materials

- lamp with shade
- acrylic paint: white, yellow & leaf green
- piece of medium-weight fabric in matching shade of yellow
- 2 fabric daisy stems
- pencil, Kraft paper & white craft glue
- all-purpose glue gun & glue sticks
- paintbrushes: round & liner
- straight pins & scissors

1. Paint lamp base white using round brush. Apply as many coats as needed for even coverage. Paint accents yellow and green using liner brush. Allow paint to dry between colors.

2. Trace lampshade on Kraft paper to make pattern. Match edge of paper to seam on shade, then roll shade while tracing outline. Add ½"/1.3cm at top and bottom and ½"/1.3cm overlap at seam. Pin pattern to fabric and cut out.

3. Apply a thin layer of white craft glue to shade. With edge of fabric matching seam on shade, wrap fabric around shade, smoothing as you go. Apply glue under seam, overlap excess and glue in place. Trim excess fabric at top and bottom of shade even with edges. Allow glue to set.

4. Separate leaves and flowers from stems. Hot-glue leaves around top and bottom edges of shade. Glue flowers over leaves. Glue flowers at base of lamp, if desired.

$$ 6-10

silk flower frame

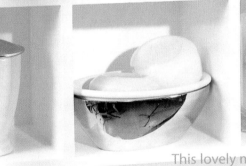

This lovely mirror will brighten even the cloudiest day! Enjoy the beauty of summer year-round with a beautiful, blooming silk floral frame.

materials
- approx. 9" x 12"/23cm x 30.5cm framed mirror
- 2 to 3 silk hydrangea stems
- all-purpose glue gun & glue sticks

Note: Some floral stems are fuller than others. If a fuller look is desired, select stems with a large number of blossoms.

1. Separate leaves and flower blossoms from stem. If petals should separate when removing flowers from stems, apply a small drop of glue between petals to hold flowers together.

2. Begin by gluing leaves to frame to create a natural background for flowers. Position leaves overlapping slightly and facing various directions.

3. Glue flowers over leaves.

$$ 6-10

coconut shell planter

Here's a unique yet simple hanging planter made from a hollowed and halved coconut shell. Hang the extra shell from a branch so birds can feast on the tasty meat.

materials

- coconut
- jute twine
- screwdriver, handsaw, drill & scissors
- pencil & tape measure
- 5" x 3"/12.5cm x 7.5cm piece heavy cardboard

1. Pierce eyes of coconut with screwdriver and empty milk. Mark coconut about 2"/5cm down from top all around. Use saw to carefully cut off top (pointed end). Drill four holes, equal distance apart, about ⅜"/1cm down from top.

2. Wrap twine 20 times around width of cardboard. Cut two 72"/183cm lengths of twine and slip both evenly through one end

of wrapped twine. Tie tightly, then cut open loops at opposite end and remove cardboard. Take another length of twine (about 1yd/.95m) and wrap around tassel about 1"/2.5cm down from top. Knot ends to secure. Untwist twine to create fuller tassel.

3. With tassel at bottom of planter, slip ends of twine through drilled holes in coconut, going from outside in. Cut another length of twine and, holding all four strands together, begin wrapping strands about 6"/15cm from their ends. Wrap about 3"/7.5cm, then fold twine ends to form loop. Wrap several more times to secure, then tie and glue twine end.

$ 1-5

Relish the intriguing texture and beauty of stones and shells by preserving their wonders on decorative balls. Group the balls in a large bowl for a distinctive display.

materials

- Styrofoam® balls
- acrylic paint in coordinating color
- stencil brush
- all-purpose glue gun & glue sticks
- smooth flat stones or seashells

1. Paint Styrofoam® ball in color that coordinates with stones or shells. Use stencil brush to work paint into crevices of foam surface.

2. Gently press stone/shell into foam to create depression. Apply glue to back of stone/shell and glue in place in recessed area. Continue in same manner gluing stones/shells one next to the other until ball is completely covered. (Shells can be glued slightly overlapping each other.)
$$ 6-10

star-shaped wreath

An all-green, star-shaped wreath formed from a twig base makes a stellar accent for a wall or door. Follow the same method to make wreaths in a variety of shapes.

Photo: VNU/Dolf Straatemeier

materials

- 10 twigs, 9"/23cm long, ¼"/6mm to ½"/1.3cm diameter
- foliage (gathered outdoors)
- floral wire, ruler & pruning shears
- all-purpose glue gun & glue sticks

Note: Be sure to keep the height and width of the wreath under 24"/61cm. If the wreath is too large, the joints may not hold when the wreath is hung.

1. Using clippers, remove any small branches jutting from sides of twigs. Trim all twigs to even 8"/20.5cm lengths.

2. Cut ten 8"/20.5cm lengths of wire. Arrange twigs end to end to form five-pointed star. Slightly overlap twigs at corners. Secure joints with wire lengths.

3. Reinforce joints with glue. Hold twigs firmly in place until glue sets.

4. Cut twenty 6"/15cm lengths of wire. Make 20 small bunches of greenery. Wire stems together just below leaves, leaving long wire ends. Trim stems to about 1"/2.5cm.

5. Starting at point of star, place bunch of wired greenery on base with leaf heads pointing upward. Tightly wrap wire ends around base to fasten. Wire second bunch to base in same manner, overlapping stems of previous bunch.

6. Continue wiring on greenery until entire wreath is covered. Examine for any gaps and fill in as needed.

$ 1-5

Capture the beauty of a summer garden! Glorious dried roses simply displayed in a box frame create an elegant specimen case.

materials

- rectangular box frame
- 6 dried roses
- pruner
- small hammer & tacks
- paper tie-on tags & pen
- white acrylic paint & wash paintbrush

Note: Pick newly opened roses from the garden, strip off any foliage, then hang them upside down in a dark, dry place to air dry.

1. Paint frame white and let dry thoroughly. If desired, remove backing from frame and cover with off-white fabric.

2. Trim rose stems to even length to fit inside frame. Position roses evenly spaced on backing about 1"/2.5cm below inside top edge and ½"/1.3cm above inside bottom edge, depending on size of frame. Group roses by type. With hammer, gently tack roses in place just below base of bloom.

3. Write variety of rose on tag in fancy script and tie to stems.

$$ 6-10

Enhance your garden with hand-crafted accent pieces. Build a path of stepping stones that spell out a friendly greeting. Showcase potted plants in a casually-styled twig box.

garden stepping stones

materials

- cement containing sand
- water bucket & mixing stick
- corrugated pizza box (about 14"/35.5cm square)
- duct tape & petroleum jelly
- twigs & shells
- rubber gloves
- piece of cardboard

Note: Use a corrugated cardboard pizza box as the mold for the stones because it is stronger and will hold its shape better than a regular box. Bear in mind that this project is messy and best done outside.

1. Reinforce pizza box with duct tape by wrapping tape all around sides. Apply thin coating of petroleum jelly to inside of box to aid in releasing stone.

2. Protect work surface and wear gloves. Mix cement in bucket according to instructions on package. Add enough water so that it is consistency of cookie dough. Pour mix into box.

3. Use straight edge of piece of cardboard to smooth top. Gently vibrate sides to release bubbles and even surface. Allow mix to set for about one hour before pressing embellishments into stone. Test with a small object first. If object sinks, allow cement to set a little while longer. Arrange objects to spell out greeting, or in design of your choice.

4. Allow stone to set for 3 to 4 days. Amount of time will vary depending on weather/temperature conditions. Peel box away from stone and set in garden.

$ 1-5

stacked twig planter

materials

- 30 twigs, 11"/28cm long, ½"/1.3cm diameter
- two 36"/91.5cm lengths of 14 gauge wire
- drill with 3/32 bit
- handsaw, pruning shears & wire cutter
- silicone glue

1. Select straight twigs and cut into uniform 11"/28cm lengths. Trim any small branches so lengths are smooth.

2. Drill holes through each twig, one ½"/1.3cm in from each end.

3. Beginning with a single twig, thread one piece of wire through one end of first twig and another piece of wire through opposite end. Move twig until it is centered on both pieces of wire. Thread 11 more twigs on wire, alternating from top to bottom, so that you have a total of 12 twigs centered on wire, forming the base of your planter.

4. Wrap wire around outside twig, and then thread wire through another twig going in a perpendicular direction on top side of base. Do this at both ends. Continue threading on twigs in alternating directions to build walls of planter until there are two twigs left. Pull wire tightly as you are threading twigs so planter is sturdy.

5. To complete planter, apply glue to wire, just above last twigs threaded. Thread last two twigs in place, pulling wire securely. Allow glue to dry, then use wire cutter to trim excess wire.

$ 1-5

These delightful ornaments will fill your home with the sweet fragrance of lavender. All you need are bunches of long-stemmed lavender, pretty silk ribbons and scissors.

materials

- approx. 30 fresh, long-stemmed lavender flowers (remove leaves from stems)
- approx. 4yds/3.7m ¼"/6mm-wide silk ribbon
- scissors

1. Cut 40"/101.5cm length of ribbon. Gather lavender in bouquet. Tie 1 end of ribbon in double knot just below flower heads (knot tight enough to hold flowers but not so tight as to damage stems).

2. Hold stems with flowers pointing downward. With free hand, draw stems down over flowers in groups of three. Space stems evenly around flower heads, hiding short end of ribbon.

3. Grasp folded stems firmly. Release three stems and start weaving ribbon alternately over and under them, reclaiming stems one at a time as you go. Continue weaving ribbon through stems, rotating ornament as needed, until flower heads are encased in woven ribbon. Use equal tension when weaving to create neat, even lattice.

4. Wrap weaving ribbon several times around base of ball and pull end through last loop to secure. Cut off excess ribbon. Cut stem ends even and insert in top of ball to finish.

$$ 6-10

Bring nature's freshness and beauty indoors! Transform scraps of garden fencing into a flowering window box to hang on an inside wall.

materials

- 7" x 15"/18cm x 38cm piece of 1 x 8 common pine (for base)
- three 8'/2.5m lattice strips
- wood glue, sandpaper & tack cloth
- wire nails, hammer & handsaw
- white acrylic primer, white acrylic paint & wash paintbrush

1. Cut lattice strips as follows: six 15"/38cm strips for front and back horizontal strips; six 1½"/26.5cm strips for back vertical strips; four 7"/18cm strips for side horizontal strips; twelve 5½"/14cm strips for front and side vertical strips. Sand rough edges smooth. Wipe with cloth.

2. Lay 2 front horizontal strips down 1½"/3.8cm apart. Intersect these with 6 front vertical strips, placing one at each end and remainder spaced evenly between. Glue in place, making sure that all pieces are straight and at right angles. Repeat this process for both sides (using 2 horizontal and 3 vertical pieces each) and for back (using 4 horizontals and 6 vertical pieces).

3. Apply primer to all wood pieces and let dry. Begin assembling box by nailing front to bottom along vertical strips perpendicular to base. Repeat for sides and back.

4. Paint entire piece with two coats white paint to finish, letting each coat dry thoroughly before applying next.

$$ 6-10

to many of us, the kitchen is the most important room of the house. Here are some fun and creative ways to give your kitchen a welcoming and comfortable atmosphere.

spearmint

Nothing rounds out a meal better than a well-dressed salad. These etched bottles are attractive enough to set on a table.

etched bottles

materials

- empty wine or other decorative bottle with cork or stopper
- glass etching cream
- clear contact paper
- tracing paper, pencil & transfer paper
- craft knife
- inexpensive or old paintbrush (set aside a brush just for using with etching cream)
- rubber gloves & protective eyewear

1. Trace patterns onto tracing paper. Cut a piece of contact paper at least 1½"/3.8cm larger all around than pattern you are using. (Etching cream will etch any glass surface it comes into contact with. The extra paper will protect the surfaces around the area you want to etch. If space is tight, use masking tape to protect your surface.)

2. Center pattern over contact paper with transfer paper in between. Go over all lines with pencil to transfer pattern to contact paper.

3. Remove backing from contact paper and press contact paper onto bottle smoothly. You can either remove backing paper as a whole sheet, or remove it gradually as you apply contact paper to bottle.

4. Cut out patterns with craft knife, then remove contact paper from cut-out areas. Be sure cut edges of contact paper remain smooth as pieces are removed.

5. Follow manufacturer's instructions to apply etching cream. Leave on glass for time indicated and rinse as directed. Remove contact paper from glass. Repeat patterns on bottle as desired.

$ 1-5

flavored oil & vinegar

materials

ingredients for rosemary oil

• olive oil

• several rosemary sprigs

ingredients for flavored red wine vinegar

• red wine vinegar

• 1 medium shallot

• 2 teaspoons pepper melange (whole red, black & white peppercorns)

ingredients for flavored white wine vinegar

• white wine vinegar

• 8 small cloves of garlic

• sprig of oregano

• 2 teaspoons black peppercorns

1. Sterilize bottles before using. Use a plain glass bottle or large jar for making the oil/vinegar and the decorative bottle for storing and serving. Carefully wash bottles and corks with warm soapy water using a bottle brush if jar/bottle necks are large enough. Carefully rinse to be sure all soap is removed. If jars/bottles fit into a pot, they can be totally submerged in water. Boil water for ten minutes. Drain bottles on a clean, dry towel. If using tall bottles, fill with boiling water and allow to stand for ten minutes. Drain as above.

2. After oil/vinegar has steeped, strain liquid into decorative bottle. Add fresh herbs or spices for decoration and seal with cork or stopper. If desired, dip cork in melted wax to seal. Bottle corks can be decorated with raffia or twine, or covered with fabric and tied with ribbon. Tie raffia or fabric leaf vines around neck of bottles.

3. Always label oil/vinegar with date and description. As these products do not use preservatives, they should be checked regularly. Discoloration or unusual odor will indicate product should be discarded. Make small batches and always refrigerate after opening.

to make rosemary oil

1. To release flavor, bruise the rosemary by gently rolling with a rolling pin or the back of a spoon.

2. Heat (do not boil) olive oil in saucepan over a low flame. Add rosemary and let sit for a few minutes. Remove rosemary and place in bottle. Pour in oil, then seal.

3. Place oil in refrigerator for 3 to 4 days to allow flavor to infuse. See Flavored Oil &Vinegar steps 2 and 3. Oil can be refrigerated for up to one month.

$ 1-5

to make flavored red wine vinegar

1. Slice shallot into thin slices. Place shallots and peppercorns in bottle.

2. Heat vinegar, then pour into bottle and seal.

3. Place bottle in a cool, dark place for 2 to 4 weeks. See Flavored Oil &Vinegar steps 2 and 3. Vinegar can be refrigerated for up to six months.

$ 1-5

to make flavored white wine vinegar

1. Place garlic, oregano and peppercorns in bottle.

2. See Flavored Red Wine Vinegar steps 2 and 3 above.

$ 1-5

Make this charming vertical wall hanging by braiding twine and gluing on tartlet pans filled with assorted dried flowers.

materials

- 3 tartlet pans, approx. 3½"/9cm diameter
- sheet moss
- assorted dried flowers & leaves
- jute twine
- glue sticks & all-purpose glue gun
- white craft glue (for flowers)

1. Glue a small piece of sheet moss to one side of each tartlet pan. (This end will become the bottom when the pan is hung, and the base on which the flowers and leaves are placed.)

2. Dip stems of flowers and leaves in white craft glue and poke into moss. Start with tallest material in back, working to smallest material in front. Let glue dry.

3. Cut three 54"/137cm lengths of twine. Hold all three together with ends even and fold in half. Wrap small piece of twine around folded lengths, about 1"/2.5cm from fold to form loop. Wrap twine 4 or 5 times around and secure with glue. Braid three twine strands together to 14"/35.5cm length. Wrap small piece of twine around end of braid in same manner as above and secure with glue. Trim ends even. Untwist twine ends for fuller "tassel."

4. Hot-glue tartlet pans to braid, equally spaced between top knot and tassel.

$$ 6-10

dish-towel apron

Dish towels make the perfect apron!
Not only are they good-looking, they're
inexpensive and easy to clean.

materials

- 1 approx. 20" x 30"/51cm x 76cm cotton dish towel
- assorted pieces of rickrack
- washable fabric glue
- 2yds/1.85m 1"/2.5cm-wide grosgrain ribbon
- tracing paper & pencil
- scissors & straight pins

Note: If purchasing rickrack, one package of each of five colors will be enough to complete apron. If using leftover pieces of rickrack, place the trim in any manner that best uses what is on hand.

1. Enlarge pattern to half width of towel. Trace pattern onto tracing paper. Fold towel in half lengthwise. Pin pattern to top and along fold line. Cut out as indicated. Remove pattern and pins. Fold cut edges under ⅜"/1cm, then ⅜"/1cm again. Pin and stitch.

2. Cut ribbon into 3 pieces, one 22"/56cm and two of equal length from remainder. Glue (or stitch) rickrack to one side of each piece of ribbon (this is optional). Glue (or stitch) rickrack to lower edge of apron.

3. Stitch neckband to top of apron on wrong side on each end (22"/56cm length). Stitch ties to each side of apron just below curved edge on wrong side.

$ 1-5

cut along this line

pin along fold

All it takes is a little paint to turn an old wooden fruit crate into a handy shelf. Sponge-stamped checks and apples give this shelf folk-art appeal.

leaf

square

apple

materials

- 2 wooden fruit crates
- acrylic primer
- acrylic paint: red, medium green, cream & brown
- waterbased protective finish
- compressed sponge & scissors
- paintbrushes: liner & wash
- hammer & small nails
- pencil, tracing & and graphite paper
- sandpaper & tack cloth

1. Remove one or both ends from second fruit box to use as "shelves." Sand rough edges and wipe with tack cloth.

2. With wash brush, paint all pieces with primer and let dry. Paint sides and back slats of box cream, shelves and top and bottom of box green with red edges.

3. Use tracing and graphite paper to transfer patterns to sponge and cut out. Dip each shape in water and squeeze out excess.

4. Use sponge shapes to stamp pattern on sides and slats of box (refer to photograph for colors and placement). Paint apple stems with liner. Dip pencil eraser in red paint and stamp dots.

5. Slip "shelves" in between sides of box and nail in place, making sure shelves are level. Brush on a coat of protective finish.

$ free

Every meal will feel like a celebration with these bright floral napkin rings. Sculpted from pieces of polymer clay, these festive table toppers will always be in season.

materials

- assorted colors of polymer clay (use leftovers)
- stylus
- cardboard tube from paper towels
- aluminum foil
- soft rubber brayer or wood dowel
- craft knife, ruler & white craft glue

1. Cut cardboard roll into 2"/5cm pieces and wrap with aluminum foil.

2. Each ring has five flowers and ten leaves. To make each flower, roll clay into pea-size balls, six for petals, and one for center. Place petal balls around center ball so that all touch. Using a soft rubber brayer or a wood dowel dusted with baby powder, roll over peas to create about ⅛"/3mm-thick flowers. To make leaves, make pea-size balls, flatten with your finger, and pinch ends to form leaf shape. Use stylus to etch lines in petals and leaves and small dots in flower centers.

3. Roll out clay to ⅛"/3mm thick. Cut strips ¼" x 8"/6mm x 20.5cm long. Wrap strips around cardboard roll, overlap ends and smooth overlap.

4. Press flowers and then leaves onto ring. Leaves and flowers may overlap.

5. Follow manufacturer's guidelines to bake clay. Allow it to cool before removing from cardboard roll. Glue on any broken pieces.

$ free

It's easy to grate and mold soap bars into attractive balls. Natural add-ins like dried herbs and essential oils give soaps a subtle fragrance and unique look.

materials

- approx. 3oz. bar of unscented bar soap
- 3 drops essential oil (should match or complement herb)
- 1½ tsps dried herbs (for example, lavender, peppermint and lemon balm)
- 1 tsp 100% vegetable oil (for example, olive or sweet almond)
- double boiler
- kitchen (vegetable) grater
- wooden spoon
- waxed paper
- 2 to 3 drops food coloring (optional)
- sheer fabric & ribbon for wrapping

1. Grate soap into top of double boiler. Add vegetable oil. Melt soap until it is soft and mushy, stirring so soap melts evenly.

2. Remove melted soap from heat. Add essential oil, herbs and food coloring and stir together.

3. When soap mixture is cool enough to work with, apply a small amount of vegetable oil to your hands and form soap into ball. If you prefer bar shape, ball can be flattened with palm of your hand or pressed into lightly-oiled cookie cutter. Allow soap to cool on waxed paper.

4. Wrap soap in fabric and tie with ribbon.

$ 1-5

soothing herbal teas

The perfect treat to help you unwind after a busy day, delicately flavored caffeine-free herbal teas calm nerves and lift spirits.

spearmint

materials

- dried herbs (for example, rosemary, lemon balm and peppermint)
- cheesecloth, lightweight muslin or lightweight interfacing
- cotton string
- small pieces of decorative/handmade paper
- specialty scissors with contoured edges
- waterproof markers
- white craft glue

1. Cut 6"/15cm circles from fabric. Place an overflowing tablespoon of herbs into center of each piece of fabric.

2. Gather fabric into a bag. Cut an 18"/46cm length of string. Leaving a 2"/5cm piece of string at the beginning, wrap string tightly around fabric several times just above herbs. Knot ends of string securely. Trim edges of fabric even.

3. Leave a 7"/18cm piece of string for teabag. Cut papers into small squares or rectangles or into shapes that describe the type of tea you have made, such as lemon or leaf shapes. You will need two of each paper shape for each bag. Glue string between two pieces of paper. With markers, write name of tea on the paper and add a decorative border.

$ 1-5

dried citrus swag

Ordinary dried fruits, like oranges and limes, combine with other natural materials to create a beautiful and aromatic swag.

materials

- twigs
- seed pods, small pinecones & whole cloves
- 20 gauge floral wire
- dried fruit: 1 orange, 1 lemon & 1 lime
- glue sticks & all-purpose glue gun

1. Gather twigs into a well-balanced bunch, wrapping wire around base of twigs as you go so bunch will be secure. Make two bunches.

2. Overlap gathered ends about 6"/15cm and wrap securely with wire.

3. Glue pods out from center.

4. Arrange fruit in center over pods and glue in place. Glue a small pinecone or clove to center of each fruit slice.

making dried fruit

1. Slice fruit into even slices approximately ¼"/6mm thick.

2. To slow dry, spread slices out on a non-rusting screen and let dry for about two weeks in a dark cool space. There is no need to turn pieces.

3. To quick dry, spread slices out on a cookie sheet. Place in oven set at 200°F/93.3°C. for about one hour (drying time will vary depending on oven). Turn slices every 15 minutes.

$ 1-5

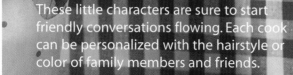

These little characters are sure to start friendly conversations flowing. Each cook can be personalized with the hairstyle or color of family members and friends.

materials

- 3 wood mixing spoons
- 3 wood beads, approx. 1¼"/3.2cm diameter
- 3 candle cups with ½"/1.3cm-diameter holders
- 18"/46cm piece ½"/1.3cm-wide ribbon
- acrylic paint: black, dark brown, orange, red, pink, white & flesh
- small pieces of sponge
- paintbrushes: liner & round
- toothpick
- white craft glue

1. With round brush, paint wood beads flesh color and candle cups white. Hair can be painted with sponges (for curly hair) or with liner brush (for straight hair and bangs).

2. Use toothpick dipped in paint for facial features. Paint eyes black, mouths white and cheeks pink. Paint beard and/or mustache with liner brush. Let dry.

3. Glue bead to top of spoon handle. Glue candle cup (Chef's hat) with open end down to top of bead (head).

4. Cut ribbon into three equal pieces. Tie each piece in a double knot around the spoon handles, just under bead (head) and glue in place.

$ 1-5

An old wooden stool becomes a decorative showpiece when painted and découpaged with a stunning floral print.

materials

- wood stool & old print
- découpage medium & acrylic primer
- acrylic paint to coordinate with print: medium shade, dark shade & brown
- wash paintbrush & toothbrush
- waterbased protective finish
- upholstery tacks & hammer
- sandpaper & tack cloth
- specialty scissors with contoured edges

1. Sand stool to prepare to receive paint. Wipe off dust with tack cloth.

2. Paint stool with primer and let dry. Then paint with one to two coats of medium shade and let dry.

3. Mix dark shade of paint with water until it is consistency of milk. Brush paint on small areas at a time, gently wiping off excess with cloth. Repeat until entire stool is covered. Thin brown paint and use toothbrush to gently splatter paint on stool.

4. Use specialty scissors to trim print to circumference approximately ½"/1.3cm smaller all around than stool top. Follow manufacturer's guidelines to apply découpage medium to print. Smooth in place, then apply two to three coats of medium to seal, letting each coat dry before applying the next.

5. Brush on a coat of protective finish. Hammer upholstery tacks around seat.

$ 1-5

towel holder

This adorable character will bring loads of personality to your kitchen. Quick paint strokes and snippets of fabric are all it takes to make this perky towel holder.

1. Drill hole 1"/2.5cm deep in center of one end of large dowel same diameter as small dowel. Drill hole ½"/1.3cm deep in wood ball (head) same diameter as small dowel. Position small dowel in hole in head and glue in place. (Other end of small dowel will slip into hole in large dowel for inserting paper towels on the completed holder.)

2. Drill a pilot hole in center bottom of plaque. Nail plaque to dowel through bottom of plaque. This is the base of holder.

3. With round brush, paint all pieces white including wood buttons for nose. Paint black spots on base and cow's head. (Spots are amorphous shapes.) With liner brush, paint comma-shaped nostrils on buttons and white dots for eyes, using photograph as your guide. Allow paint to dry thoroughly.

4. Glue buttons (nose) to head. Paint wrinkle lines in black just above nose as pictured. Drill two small holes (same diameter as wire) on each side of head. Wrap wire around a pencil to curl. Cut wire in half and glue one piece into each hole.

5. Trace pattern for ears on tracing paper. Pin pattern to felt and cut out two pieces. Glue ears to either side of head. Tie ribbon through bell and then tie bell around neck. Place head on holder.

$$ 6-10

ear

toys for tots

Combine playtime with creativity! This chapter is filled with lots of fun craft ideas to inspire your young ones' imaginations.

Children will delight in this miniature fantasy world filled with all their favorite sports equipment. Shake the globe to see a blizzard of glittering flakes.

materials

- small pieces of polymer clay: white, red, yellow, brown & tan
- small baby food jar
- paintbrush & acrylic paint in desired color
- silicone glue & white craft glue (optional)
- ruler, water & glitter

1. Wash jar, remove labels and paint jar lid. If paint does not stick, add a few drops of white craft glue to help it adhere. Measure height of jar and size pieces to fit.

2. Form round, flat circle of clay, about ¼"/6mm thick and about ¼"/6mm smaller all around than jar opening for base.

3. Shape clay into sports balls, such as a baseball and football. Make a tennis racket, baseball glove or bat. Make small indentations in base. Set balls and other decorations into base. Be sure pieces are sticking together.

4. Bake clay, following manufacturer's guidelines. (If needed, use silicone glue to glue pieces together.)

5. Glue base centered on inside of jar lid. Let glue to dry. Fill jar full with water. Add glitter. Add more water if needed to cover clay. Dry inside edge of lid and top edge of jar. Apply a small amount of silicone glue along top edge of jar. Slip pieces inside jar and screw closed. Do not turn jar over until glue is dry.

$ free

Start off family fun day with this modern update on a classic game. The baseball motifs are perfect for a boy, while the "love and kisses" will please a little girl.

materials
- foam sheets, 9" x 12"/23cm x 30.5cm: for girl's game: 1 each in white, light pink, dark pink & red; for boy's game: 2 in white; 1 each in green, brown & red
- white craft glue
- scissors
- ruler
- tracing paper, lightweight cardboard & pencil

1. Cut a 9"/23cm square of white foam for base of game board. Cut nine 2¾"/7cm squares (green for boys, light pink for girls). Position squares in three evenly spaced rows on base and glue in place.

2. Make five of each game piece: Transfer patterns for each game piece onto tracing paper. Glue paper to cardboard and cut out to make templates. Trace templates on foam sheets (balls on white, ball details on red, bats on brown, large hearts on red, small hearts on white, and "X" kisses on dark pink). You will need two bats, two kiss pieces, and two ball details for each game piece. Cut out all pieces.

3. Glue small heart to center of large heart. Glue details to each ball. Criss-cross two bats or two kiss pieces to make game pieces.

$ 1-5 (each game)

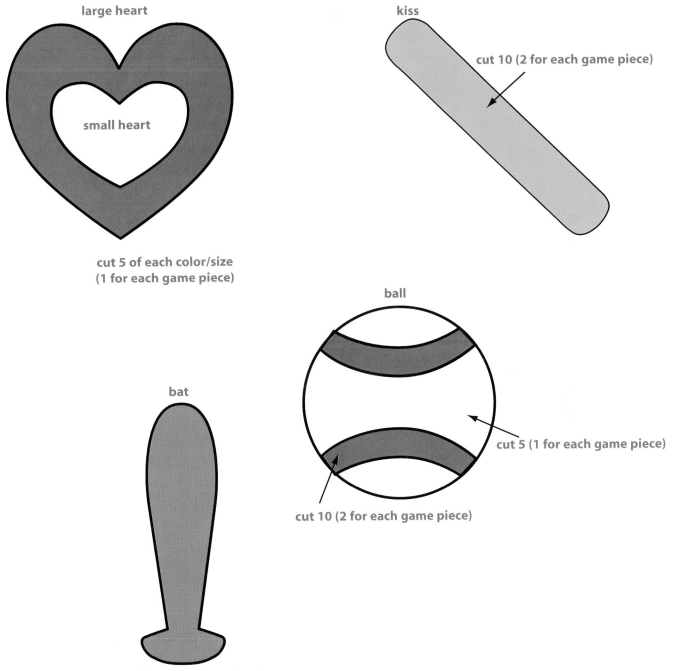

large heart

small heart

cut 5 of each color/size
(1 for each game piece)

kiss

cut 10 (2 for each game piece)

ball

cut 5 (1 for each game piece)

cut 10 (2 for each game piece)

bat

cut 10 (2 for each game piece)

Strike up the band! Spark your child's musical interest with bright and snazzy instruments made from items found around the home.

jazzy drum

materials

- small trash can, flowerpot or large oatmeal container
- large pieces felt or paper in assorted bright colors (amounts will vary depending on size of container used)
- scrap of vinyl tablecloth or shower curtain
- buttons, decorative trim, large rubber band & white craft glue
- pair of wooden chopsticks & 2 wooden

beads, approx. ¾"/2cm in diameter
- acrylic paint in bright colors & paintbrush

1. Cut a piece of felt/paper to fit sides and bottom of container. Glue in place. Cut triangles of felt/paper in assorted colors and glue along top and bottom edges of drum.
2. Cut a round piece of vinyl 2"/5cm larger all around than top opening of drum. Place rubber band around top of drum, about 1½"/3.8cm down from edge. Slip

edges of vinyl circle under rubber band and pull taut. Trim edges even.

3. Glue trim around edges of vinyl, covering rubber band. Glue buttons on triangles.

4. Paint chopsticks and wood beads and let dry. Insert sticks into bead holes and glue in place for drumsticks.

$ 1-5

groovy guitar

materials

- tissue box (one large enough to hold about 175 tissues)
- 25"/63.5cm-long cardboard tube (from wrapping paper)
- cardboard (optional)
- large pieces of felt or paper in assorted bright colors
- 2 wood craft sticks
- 3 rubber bands
- white craft glue
- 2yds/1.85m gold cord
- ⅓yard/3.5m gold trim
- coping saw & scissors
- scraps of 1½"/3.8cm-wide ribbon

1. Cut hole in center of one short end of box, ⅛"/3mm larger than tube all around. If opening on top of tissue box is too large,

cut a piece of cardboard the same size as box top and cut out 3½"/9cm circle from center. Glue cardboard to box top.

2. Cut pieces of colorful felt or paper to fit sides, ends, bottom and top of tissue box and glue in place. Glue strips of ribbon alternating with gold cord to cover tube. Apply glue to bottom end of tube and insert in hole in box end. Apply glue around hole and hold in place until glue sets. Glue trim around opening on box top.

3. Cut notches along one side of each stick. Notches should be spaced about ½"/1.3cm apart, beginning 1"/2.5cm from each end of each stick.

4. Apply glue to ends and un-notched edges of sticks. Glue sticks in a parallel position about 1"/2.5cm above and 1"/2.5cm below opening in box top, with notches facing outside. Allow glue to dry completely. Loop one rubber band around notches on first stick, then gently stretch and loop around corresponding notches on second stick. Repeat to attach remaining rubber bands.

$ 1-5

krazy kaleidoscope

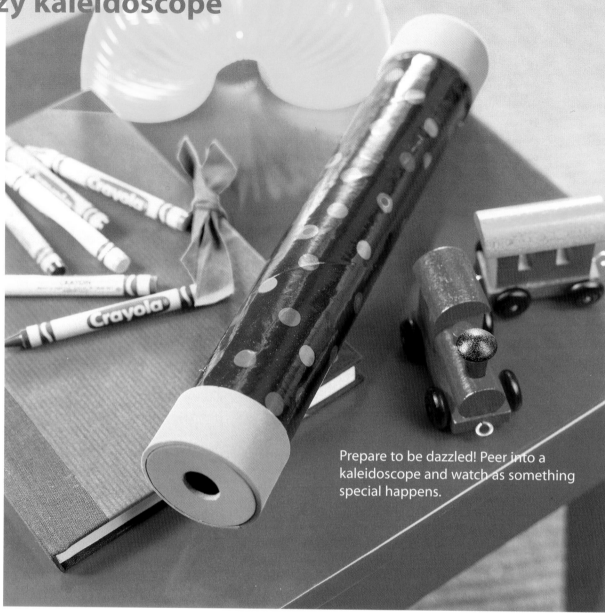

Prepare to be dazzled! Peer into a kaleidoscope and watch as something special happens.

materials

- cardboard tube from paper towel
- wrapping paper, white craft glue & craft foam
- clear plastic beads in assorted colors (pony, flowers, stars, etc.)
- piece of cardboard, 9½" x 4⅛"/24.3cm x 10.5cm
- piece of aluminum foil (large enough to cover both sides of cardboard)
- 2"/5cm square of Mylar
- 2"/5cm square of plastic (cut from lid of food container)

1. Cover outside of tube with wrapping paper. Cover cardboard front and back with aluminum foil. Fold foil-covered cardboard lengthwise into three equal 1⅜"/3.5cm sections and tape to form triangle.

2. Cut a 1¾"/4.5cm diameter circle from craft foam and plastic. Cut a 1⅝"/4cm circle from Mylar. Cut a ½"/1.3cm-diameter circle from center of foam disc. Cut two strips of craft foam, 1⅛" x 7"/3cm x 18cm.

3. Glue foam disc to one end of tube. Wrap strip of foam around this end, matching edges, and glue in place. Trim away any excess foam.

4. Slip cardboard triangle into tube, easing it down to foam-covered end. Apply glue to edges of Mylar circle and slip into tube until it rests over cardboard triangle. Allow glue to dry.

5. Fill hollow end of tube about halfway with assorted beads, then glue plastic circle on top. Wrap other strip of foam around this end, matching edges, and glue in place. Allow glue to dry.

6. Facing light source, look through eyehole in foam disc and rotate tube.

$ 1-5

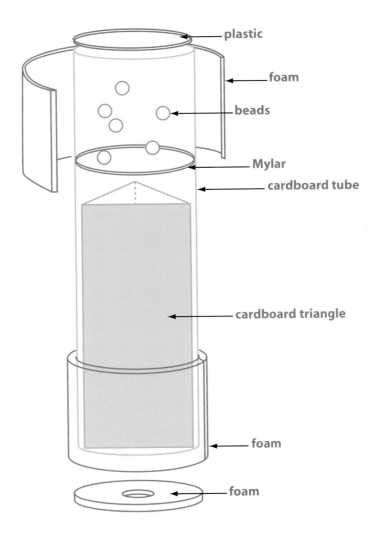

plastic

foam

beads

Mylar

cardboard tube

cardboard triangle

foam

foam

animal face masks

Looking for a quick disguise? With these masks, kids can create a whole cast of wild animal characters for loads of make-believe fun.

Note: Masks stand away from the face, so cutting a breathing space at the nose and mouth is optional.

terrific tiger

materials

- white craft glue
- scissors & craft knife
- pencil, graphite paper & lightweight cardboard
- foam sheets, 9" x 12"/23cm x 30.5cm: one

each in orange, black, white, light pink, dark pink & green (use leftovers for small pieces)
- 1yd/.95m ⅛"/3mm-wide ribbon

1. Enlarge pattern to size on photocopier. Make an extra copy to cut apart to make smaller pattern pieces.

2. Cut an 8"/20.5cm-diameter circle from orange foam. Place pattern over circle with graphite paper in between. Trace outline of eyes. Cut out eyes with craft knife.

3. Use graphite paper to transfer patterns to foam. Make two orange ears with light pink centers, one light pink mouth and dark pink nose, two green eyes, and a white muzzle with black spots. For black foam pieces, glue pattern pieces to cardboard and cut out to make templates (you only need one of each stripe). Trace templates on black foam with light-colored pencil. Cut out all pieces. Cut out center of green eyes with craft knife. Glue pieces in place, referring to photograph for placement.

4. Cut ribbon in half and glue to sides of mask for ties.

$ 1-5

funny bunny

materials

- white craft glue
- scissors & craft knife
- pencil, graphite paper & lightweight cardboard
- foam sheets, 9" x 12"/ 23cm x 30.5cm: two white; one each in light pink, dark pink & black (use leftovers for small pieces)
- 1yd/.95m ⅛"/3mm-wide ribbon

1. Enlarge pattern to size on photocopier. Make an extra copy to cut apart to make smaller pattern pieces.

2. Cut an 8"/20.5cm-diameter circle of white foam for base of mask. Place pattern over circle with graphite paper in between and trace outline of eyes. Cut out eyes with craft knife.

3. Use graphite paper to transfer patterns for facial details to foam. Make two white ears with light pink centers, two light pink cheeks, one dark pink nose, and one black mouth. For black foam pieces, glue pattern pieces to cardboard and cut out to make templates. Trace templates on black foam with light-colored pencil or ballpoint pen. Cut out all pieces with scissors. Glue pieces in place, referring to photograph for placement.

4. Cut ribbon in half and glue to sides of mask for ties.

$ 1-5

excellent elephant

materials

- white craft glue
- scissors & craft knife
- pencil & graphite paper
- foam sheets, 9" x 12"/ 23cm x 30.5cm: two purple; one each in light pink, dark pink & white (use leftovers for small pieces)
- 1yd/.95m ⅛"/3mm-wide ribbon

1. Enlarge pattern to size on photocopier. Make an extra copy to cut apart to make smaller pattern pieces.

2. Cut an 8"/20.5cm diameter circle of purple foam for base of mask. Place pattern over circle with graphite paper in between and trace outline of eyes. Cut out eyes with craft knife.

3. Use graphite paper to transfer patterns for facial details to foam. Make two purple ears with dark pink centers, one purple trunk with dark pink tip, two light pink cheeks, and two white tusks. Cut out all pieces with scissors. Glue pieces in place, referring to photograph for placement.

4. Cut ribbon in half and glue to sides of mask for ties.

$ 1-5

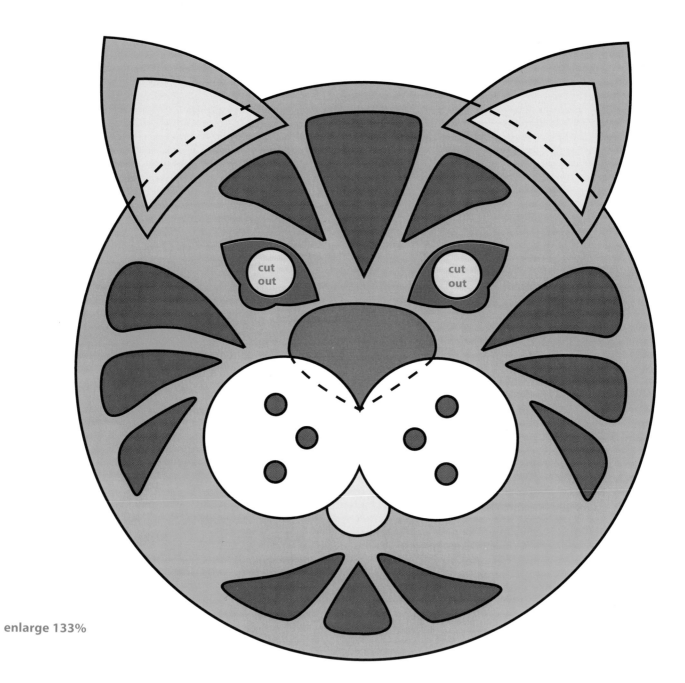

enlarge 133%

enlarge 133%

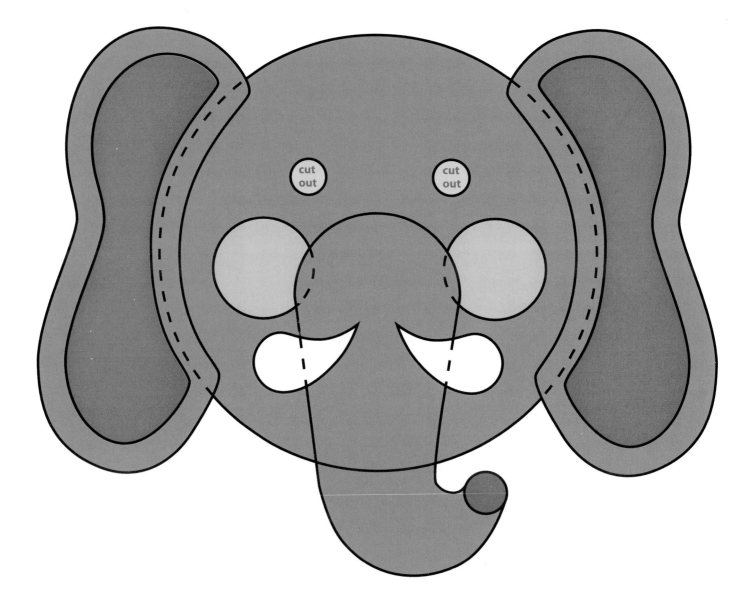

enlarge 177%

Playtime becomes learning time with this wonderful jigsaw puzzle made from a recycled road map. The puzzle comes with a handy tote bag for on-the-go fun.

materials

- map of the United States of America
- poster board (slightly larger than map)
- spray adhesive & white craft glue
- scissors
- 2 sheets of craft foam in desired color, 11" x 17"/28cm x 43cm
- plastic lacing & large needle

1. Cut map into segments along state borders. Follow spray adhesive manufacturer's guidelines to adhere map pieces to poster board. (If desired, paper glue can be used instead of spray adhesive.) Cut out individual states.

2. To make tote bag, cut two 11" x 14"/28cm x 35.5cm pieces and two 1½" x 11"/3.8cm x 28cm pieces from craft foam. Place large pieces of foam one on top of the other. With needle, pierce foam ¼"/6mm in from edges on three sides (not on top), making holes ½"/1.3cm apart.

3. Use plastic lacing and needle to stitch craft foam pieces together. Knot end of lace at beginning and end to secure.

4. Glue strips of foam to center top of tote to make handles. Place each end of handle about 4½"/11.5cm in from side edges.

$$ 6-10

More buddy than beast! Let your kids' imaginations run wild with this friendly dragon puppet.

Note: Puppet can be any color, depending on the color of the sock you use. Felt colors can be changed to contrast with sock. Sock could also be dyed to color of your choice.

materials

- 1 ladies crew sock
- felt pieces: 6" x 6"/15cm x 15cm green; 3" x 4"/7.5cm x 10cm red; 4" x 10"/10cm x 25.5cm pink; 1" x 2"/2.5cm x 5cm black & 1½" x 2½"/3.8cm x 6.5cm white
- 1 skein 6-strand embroidery thread & #5 chenille needle
- 4" x 10"/10cm x 25.5cm piece of lightweight cardboard
- two ½"/1.3cm green pompoms
- tracing paper, pencil, white craft glue & scissors

1. Trace all patterns onto tracing paper. Referring to photograph for colors, cut two each of spine and eye pieces and one each of mouth and flame. Pin patterns to felt and cut out. Tape mouth pattern to cardboard and cut out. Score center line of cardboard with scissors blade and fold in half for mouth piece.

2. With heel of sock facing up, slip folded cardboard into toe of sock. Toe seam of sock should be straight across cardboard on underside of sock. Slip point of scissors blade between folded cardboard and slit sock open, going from edge to edge of mouth piece.

3. Remove cardboard, unfold and center over pink felt. Glue cardboard to felt and allow glue to dry (felt will be inside of mouth). Fold in half and slip back into opening, matching edges of felt with sock. Pin to hold. Using needle and floss, blanket-stitch mouth to sock (see page 93).

4. Glue flame to inside of mouth along fold line. Glue spine pieces, one next to the other, starting at heel and going forward towards toe. Glue black circles to white circles for eyes, then glue eyes in place. Glue pompoms for nose at tip of mouth.

$ 1-5

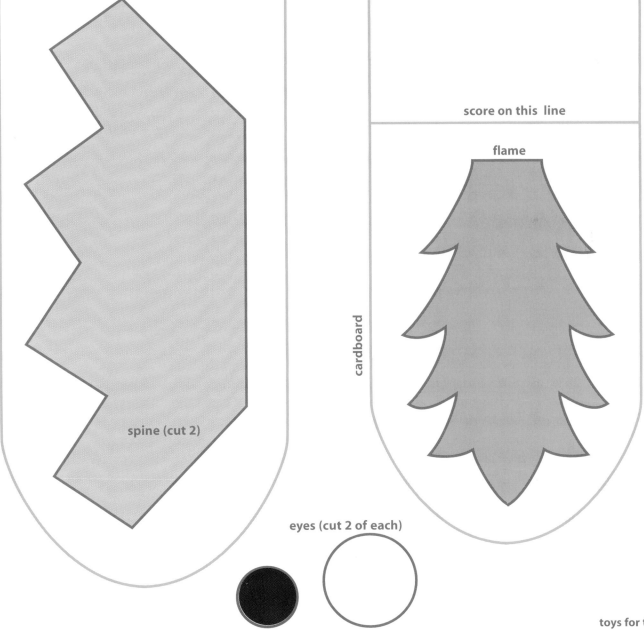

mouth

spine (cut 2)

score on this line

flame

cardboard

eyes (cut 2 of each)

fun town play mat

Are your little ones all revved up with no place to go? Let them use their toy trains to explore this fantasy village.

materials

- 36"/91.5cm square of blue felt for background
- ⅓yd/30.5cm black felt for roads
- felt and/or fabric scraps in assorted colors
- dimensional fabric paint in assorted colors
- approx. 4yds/3.7m paper-backed fusible web
- iron & ironing board
- tracing paper, pencil & lightweight cardboard
- scraps of colorful rickrack
- fabric glue & white craft glue
- scissors

Note: Patterns and/or measurements are given for all pieces shown on this mat. Your mat can be any combination of houses, stores, trees and roads that you like, in colors of your choice.

1. Trace patterns onto tracing paper. In addition to these pieces, outline the following onto tracing paper: 5"/12.5cm-square houses; 1"/2.5cm-square house and door windows; 2½" x 3"/6.5cm x 7.5cm store windows; 1½" x 2½"/3.8cm x 6.5cm doors; 1" x 3½"/2.5cm x 9cm store signs. Cut out pattern pieces. Glue pattern pieces to cardboard and cut out to make templates. Roads are 4"/10cm wide and can be length/width of mat or intersect at various points.

2. Follow manufacturer's guidelines to fuse web to black felt. Cut out roads and arrange on mat. Remove paper backing and fuse in place. Fuse web to remaining

store roof

house roof

bush

sun

star

tree

fence can be extended by adding pickets

fence

felt/fabric pieces. Trace templates for houses, trees, fences, etc. to paper side of fusible web. Use different colors for buildings, windows and doors. Use green for treetops and bushes and brown for tree trunks. For variety, turn templates over to other side and draw patterns in reverse (this will work for tree tops, trunks, bushes and house roofs). Extend fence by repeating pattern next to one already traced.

3. Cut out pieces. Fuse windows and doors to houses/stores and fruit to trees. Arrange pieces on mat, adding, removing or changing them around as desired. When arrangement is complete, remove paper backing and fuse pieces in place.

4. Paint details when all fusing is complete. Paint dashed lines on roads to separate lanes. Paint names on store signs.

5. Glue rickrack to edges of mat and let dry.

$$ 6-10

rainbow windsock

Make a colorful windsock to catch the breeze outside your home. Hang it from a tree branch, flagpole, or anyplace where it can blow freely in the wind.

materials
- two 5"/12.5cm embroidery hoops (inner hoops only)
- nylon fabric: 11" x 16¾"/28cm x 42.5cm piece in yellow; 15" x 16¾"/38cm x 42.5cm piece in blue
- 1½ yds/1.4m 1½"/3.8cm-wide rainbow-striped ribbon
- washable fabric glue
- pinking shears
- 4yds/3.7m cord
- grommets & grommet setting tool

1. Along short edge of blue fabric, starting 1"/2.5cm down from top, lightly mark lines ½"/1.3cm apart. Use pinking shears to cut streamers, leaving 1"/2.5cm-wide band at top.

2. Cut three 16¾"/42.5cm lengths of ribbon. Glue one piece of ribbon across center (16¾"/42.5cm width) of yellow fabric. Glue second piece of ribbon 1"/2.5cm down from top edge of fabric. Glue top edge (1"/2.5cm band) of blue fabric 1"/2.5cm up from bottom edge of yellow fabric. Glue last piece of ribbon over blue band, just above streamers.

3. Wrap embellished fabric around hoop (ribbon should be horizontal) and mark where fabric overlaps. Remove hoop and glue yellow fabric along edge (at marking) to make tube. Allow glue to dry.

4. Slip a hoop in at top and bottom ends of tube. Wrap yellow fabric around top and bottom hoop so that edges of ribbon are at edges of hoops and streamers hang downward.

5. Insert four grommets evenly spaced ¾"/2cm down from top edge of windsock. Cut four 1yd/.95m lengths of cord. Starting from inside, slip one length through each grommet and knot end to hold in place. Knot four lengths together about 9"/23cm from top of windsock, and again at ends. Trim ends to even.

$ 1-5

the craft tool kit is a collection of basic tools and supplies which, when combined and used with other simple materials, allows you to craft beautiful finished objects. We are not suggesting that you go out and buy all of these items at once, but rather that they should be accumulated over time as needed. Ask for recommendations when purchasing tools like scissors and always try to buy the best quality that you can afford. With proper care and maintenance, some of these tools can last a lifetime.

For any of the products mentioned, always follow the manufacturer's instructions for proper and safe usage. Although some products may appear to be the same, each may in fact require a different method of application and handling.

Bear in mind that creative inspiration can strike at any moment. With a well-stocked tool kit, you will always be prepared.

1. Brush Cleaner Having quality brushes on hand is important, and the only way to make them last is to keep them clean. A brush cleaner for acrylic paint will keep your brushes in top condition.

2. Compressed Sponges When purchased, these sponges are like a thick piece of paper. Patterns and shapes can be drawn on them with a pencil or waterproof marker, then cut out with scissors. Dip the sponge in water to inflate. Wring out the excess water before dipping the sponge in paint.

3. Stencil Brush In addition to being used for stenciling, these brushes can be used to create textural effects.

4. Angular Shader The bristles on these brushes are angled, making them ideal for painting hard to reach areas, such as corners.

5. Round Brush Use these brushes to fill in small and large areas and to make decorative strokes. The amount of pressure exerted on the brush will change the width of the strokes.

6. Spotter This brush is used for fine detail work, such as painting facial features.

7. Liner As the name suggests, liners are for painting lines of equal or varied thicknesses, depending on the amount of pressure applied. When working with this brush, paint should be thinned slightly to allow for a smooth flow.

8. Wash Use this brush for basecoating and applying finishes.

9. Foam Brush Use a foam brush to apply découpage medium and to coat broad, smooth areas with paint.

paints and finishes

1. Primer Primer is used to prepare clean, dry surfaces to receive paint. It seals porous surfaces and allows acrylic paint to be applied smoothly. Check the product label to ensure the primer is suitable for the surface you are working on.

2. Varnishes/Finishes These provide a protective coating for most craft surfaces, excluding fabrics. Select a product according to the look desired: "matte" for a flat finish, "gloss" for a shiny one, and "satin" for a smooth, soft finish. All are water-resistant, with products designed for interior and exterior purposes.

3. Découpage Medium This is used as both a glue and finish with fabric and paper cutouts on hard surfaces, such as wood and papier mâché.

4. Crackle Medium This medium gives surfaces an aged and "crackled" look. Crackles can be fine or large, depending

on the product chosen and method of application.

5. Textile Medium Textile medium keeps paint soft and flexible after it has dried onto fabric. Check the product label for mixing and application.

6. Candle Painting Medium This product allows paint to adhere to candle surfaces. Check product label for mixing and application.

7. Fabric Paint Applied directly from the bottle through a precision tip, these paints create a dimensional appearance. Check the product labels for specifications.

8. Acrylic Paint These can be used for painting, sponging and for creating various textural finishes on a variety of surfaces. They are available in many colors, including metallics, and can be combined with different mediums for specific applications.

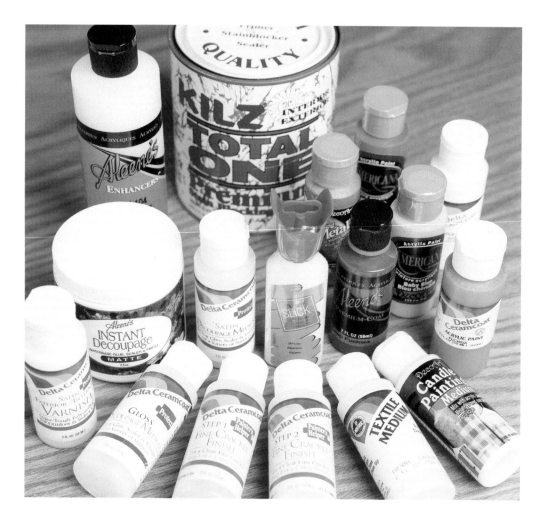

1. Hammer Use hammers for driving nails and pulling them out.

2. Tack Cloth After sanding, gently wipe surfaces with a tack cloth to remove residue, dirt and dust before painting.

3. Wire Cutter Use this tool to cut wire of various gauges.

4. Hand Drill Use a hand drill to drill holes in wood, soft metal and some plastics. Select a drill with a choice of bit sizes.

5. Coping Saw This saw is used for decorative and precision cutting. The blade is thin and can be easily replaced.

6. Needle-nose Pliers These pliers are used for bending wire and jewelry making. The tapered end allows for grasping of small items.

7. Flat-nose Pliers Use these pliers for bending or gripping wire. They are ideal for precision crafting.

8. Sandpaper Available in a variety of grits from coarse to smooth, sandpaper is used to smooth rough edges and to prepare a surface for painting. When sanding wood, always sand with the wood grain.

9. Handsaw Look for a multi-purpose handsaw with a comfortable grip and interchangeable blades.

10. Pruner Use a pruner to cut stems and small branches of both live and dried floral materials.

11. Screwdriver Screwdrivers are available in Standard for screws with slotted heads, and Phillips for Phillips head screws, as well as in different widths and lengths.

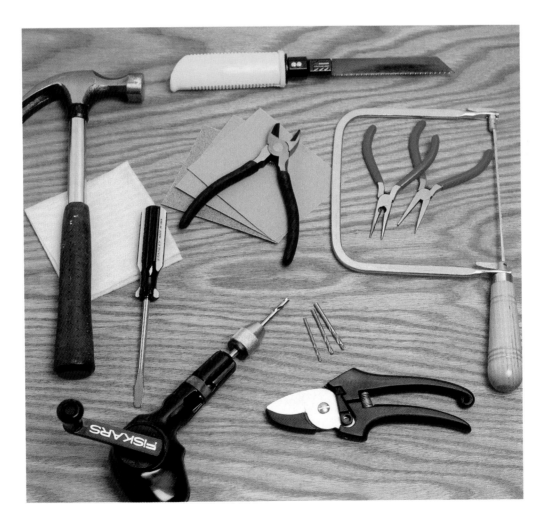

scissors and cutters

1. Fabric Scissors Use these scissors for cutting trims and fabrics of various weights. Keep separate scissors for fabric and paper.

2. Paper Scissors Paper scissors are used to cut paper, cardboard and foam sheets.

3. Pinking Shears Use pinking shears to finish fabric edges and seams. Pinked (or zigzag) edges also add a decorative touch to fabric and craft materials.

4. Rotary Cutter and Blades Cutters can be used to cut paper, fabric, cardboard, plus a variety of other craft materials. There are different blades available to create straight or decorative edges.

5. Craft Knife Use a craft knife to cut lightweight materials, such as cloth, paper or acetate. This tool is best for cutting precise and detailed shapes.

6. Precision Scissors This tool is used for embroidery and other detail cutting of fabric.

7. Specialty Scissors Decorative or contoured edge scissors are available in a wide variety of patterns, and are great tools for making cards and stationery.

1. Glue Gun This is one of the most useful tools in your craft tool kit. Select an all-purpose glue gun, preferably one which has different heat settings, interchangeable tips and can be used with a variety of glue sticks (for example, all-purpose, wood and fabric). The glue will set quickly, so it is important to plan your project carefully. Always read the tool manufacturer's guidelines for safe handling.

2. Wood Glue Specifically formulated for crafting with wood, these glues can be sanded and painted when dry.

3. White Craft Glue An all-purpose craft glue is suitable for use on most surfaces.

Some are thicker and tackier than others for gluing hard-to-hold objects. Most glues dry crystal clear—check the product label before using.

4. Paper Glue Paper glues are designed especially for paper crafting. Many allow for repositioning of pieces and prevent papers from curling.

5. Fabric Glue Use this product to glue fabric appliqués, laces and trims to fabric. Fabric glues remain flexible when dry, and many are washable. Refer to the product label for product specifications.

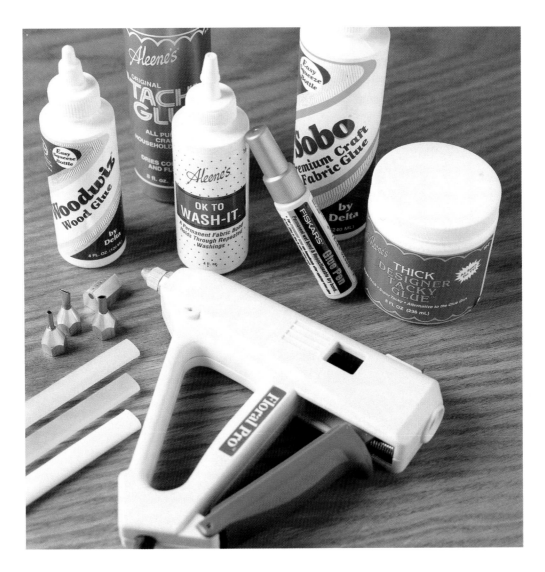

stitchery

1. Knitting Needles These are available in a variety of sizes. Check knitting patterns material lists for proper needle size to use for each project. Needles are sized according to diameter in millimeters. In the United States, they are also given a number size ranging from 0 to 15, 0 being the smallest.

2. Needles Hand needles are available in a variety of types and sizes—the one to use depends on the individual project. *Crewel needles* are used for embroidery, and have sharp points and large eyes for easy threading. *Chenille needles* are also sharp, but are larger than crewel needles. They can be used for embroidery with heavier threads and yarn. *Tapestry needles* are about the same size as chenille needles, except they are blunt-tipped. Use tapestry needles for needlepoint and counted thread embroidery. Check material lists for proper type and size of needle to use for each project. Keep in mind that the larger the needle number, the shorter and finer the needle.

protective gear

1. Rubber Gloves Although many of the products used in crafting can be cleaned up with soap and water, rubber gloves can still be worn to protect your hands. Always wear gloves when recommended by product manufacturer.

2. Goggles An excellent safety precaution, protective eyewear should be worn when using hand or power tools, and when working with materials that might be irritating to the eyes.

miscellaneous

1. Transfer Paper/Graphite Paper Transfer and graphite paper are used to transfer a pattern or drawing to another surface, such as paper, wood, glass or ceramics. Unlike carbon paper, transfer paper lines can be erased with any eraser and washes off glass and ceramics. Transferred lines also can be painted over. Papers are available in light and dark colors to contrast with surfaces.

2. Glass Etching Cream The look of frosted and etched glass can be created with this product. It is of utmost importance to follow product instructions for safe usage and to achieve desired effects.

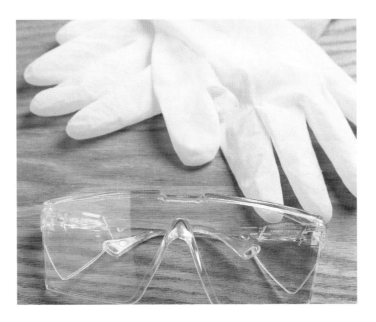

101 craft resources

Thanks to the following companies for providing some of the materials and supplies used in this book.

Adhesive Technologies
3 Merrill Industrial Drive
Hampton, NH 03842-1995
(800) 458-3486
www.adhesivetech.com
Glue gun

DecoArt
P.O. Box 386
Stanford, KY 40484
(606) 365-3193
www.decoart.com
Paints and candle painting medium.

Delta Technical Coatings, Inc.
2550 Pellissier Place
Whittier, CA 90601
(562) 695-7969
www.deltacrafts.com
Paints, crackle medium, découpage
medium, varnish, glues.

Duncan Enterprises
5673 East Shields Avenue
Fresno, CA 93727
(559) 291-4444
www.duncancrafts.com
Paints, decoupage medium,
primer, glues.

Fiskars, Inc.
305 84th. Avenue South
Wausau, WI 54401
(715) 842-2091
www.fiskars.com
Scissors, cutters, tools.

Loew-Cornell
563 Chestnut Avenue
Teaneck, NJ 07666-2490
(201) 836-7070
www.loew-cornell.com
Paintbrushes

To my parents,
who have always nurtured and supported
my creative spirit in every way possible.

Julia Bernstein has been involved in a wide variety of aspects in the craft industry. A versatile designer, her projects have been featured in most popular women's and crafting magazines as well as various craft kits, leaflets and booklets. Julia's skills are many and *101 Crafts under $10* has allowed her to showcase a number of them. She resides in New York City.